Museu de Arte Moderna Rio de Janeiro Architecture and Construction

Museu de Arte Moderna Rio de Janeiro Architecture and Construction

Gávea INVESTIMENTOS   AAA   Cobogó

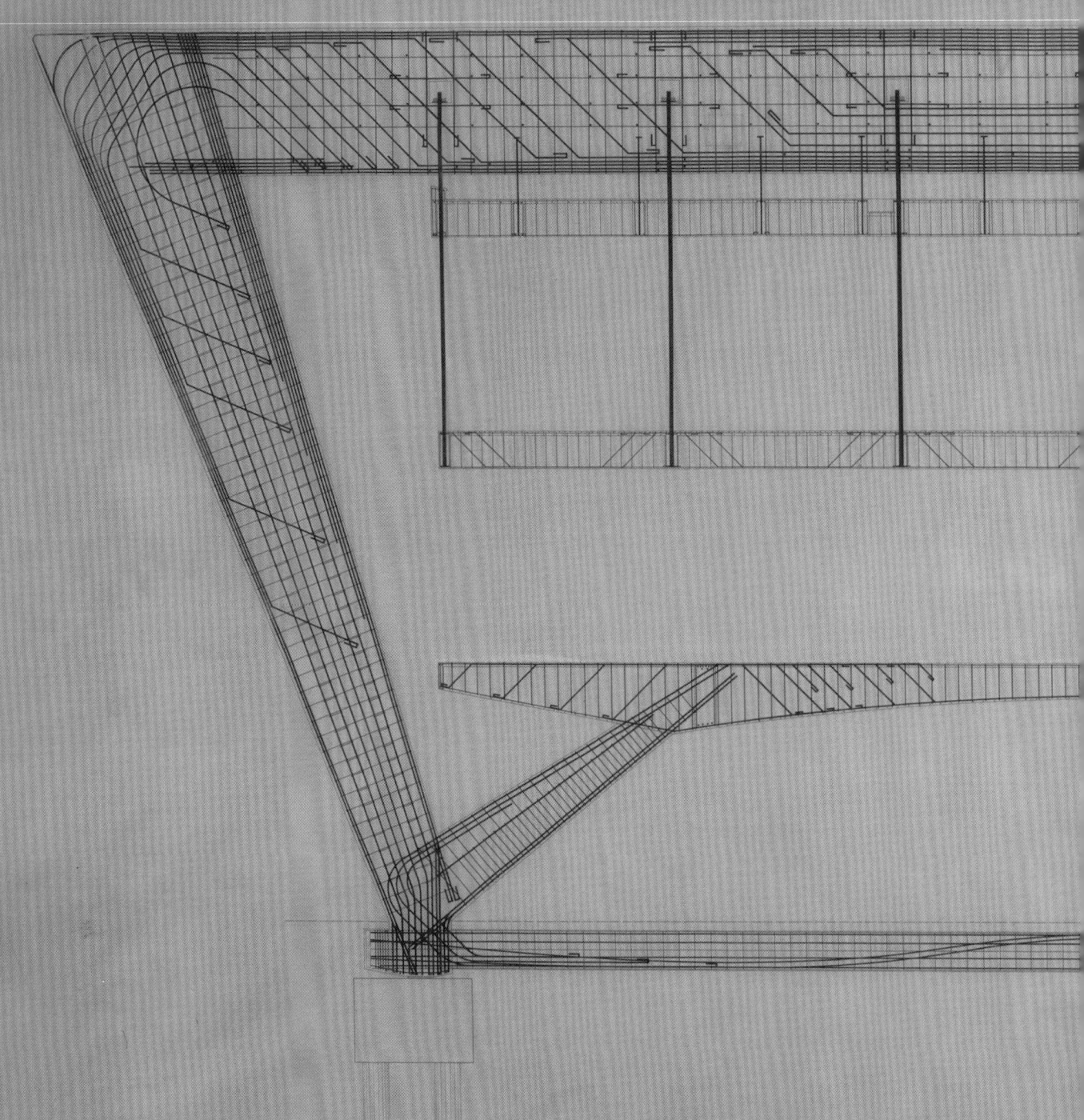

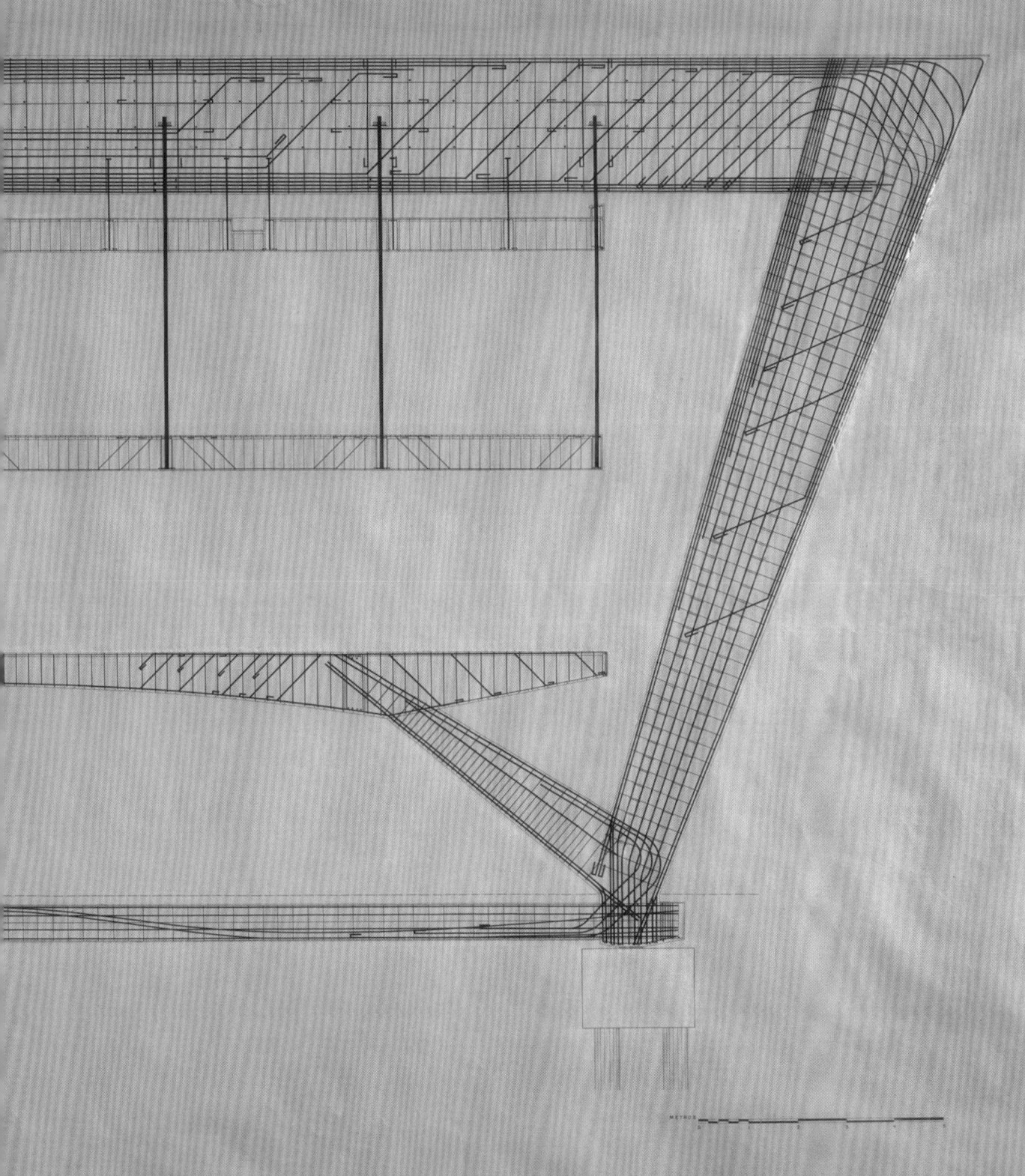

Throughout the course of its history, the Museu de Arte Moderna do Rio de Janeiro has always been mindful of its role and performance within the society for which it was created. As a *Carioca* institution *par excellence*, the MAM has never shied from historical participation in Brazilian art's key moments or, indeed, in those of our city.

In addition to being a space for creating and reflecting on art and the city, the MAM is also part of a history broader than that of the institution itself. Located in one of modern Brazilian architecture's most representative buildings, overlooking one of the world's most famous postcard views, our museum successfully articulates its everyday activities with the beauties of art and nature. From the inception of his project, architect Affonso Eduardo Reidy was intent on bequeathing to the city an institution whose seat is, to this day, in and of itself, a monument to the modern idea of a Brazil in permanent transformation. With its simultaneously Brazilian and universal architecture, Reidy succeeded in transforming the Museu de Arte Moderna do Rio de Janeiro into a museum that showcases not only Rio but all of its visitors. For more than fifty years, its building has been a landmark for architects and tourists from every corner of the world.

The finest way that the MAM was able to find of giving something back to all those who, throughout its history, have admired its buildings and vistas in one way or another was to prepare a publication about the museum's construction that would have visual appeal as well as research value. This partnership with Gávea Investimentos is the result of a joint effort to recast Rio as an active cultural and institutional agent after a period of slumber. Finally, with this book, the Museu de Arte Moderna do Rio de Janeiro offers the public a fundamental piece of the history of the nation's architecture and that of its memory.

Carlos Alberto Gouvêa Chateaubriand
President
Museu de Arte Moderna do Rio de Janeiro

For a forward-looking investment management firm, there is nothing more important than investing in the design of an individual, idiosyncratic culture. In collaborating with the publication of a book about the architecture and construction of the Museu de Arte Moderna do Rio de Janeiro, Gávea Investimentos is also investing in the culture of Rio and Brazil by means of a direct connection with our city's population and its principal museum.

Having Gávea Rock as one of the inspirations for our company's name, the partnership with the MAM now allows us to approach another one of the city's regions – Guanabara Bay and its perfect fusion of the Sugar Loaf's hills and the museum's pilotis. The marriage between modernity and nature, between the solidity of concrete and the lightness of its forms also symbolizes our participation in this project.

In recording the museum's historical role, it is also our intention to underscore the central role that Rio played and will continue to play within the nation's cultural context. A book on the architecture of Affonso Eduardo Reidy – and specifically about the Museu de Arte Moderna do Rio de Janeiro's buildings – is undoubtedly a lasting contribution towards his monumental endeavor as the portrait of a time in which the spirit of development and modernity was spreading throughout all the sectors of society. Then as now, it is crucial that the population of Rio embrace its institutions, its landscape and its culture in order to present its most vital countenance to Brazil and to the world.

Gávea Investimentos believes that the idea that disseminating one of the most remarkable moments in the cultural history of Rio de Janeiro and Brazil through a publication of quality such as this one – available in both Portuguese and English – represents a firm step in the merging of its identity with that of our city and, especially, with that of our art.

Gávea Investimentos

Foreword **Luiz Camillo Osorio** 14

Descriptive Memorial **Affonso Eduardo Reidy** 20

The Images 28
Razing, Landfill and Occupation of the Tract 30
Preparing for Construction: Piles, Foundations and Structures 40
Construction of the School Building 52
Construction of the Exhibition Building 76
School Building, Exhibition Building and Theater: the Project's Conclusion 100

A Museum Through **Ana Luiza Nobre** 110

Statement **Paulo Mendes da Rocha** 118

Photographic Essay **Vicente de Mello** 124

Chronology 138

Biographical Note 142

Image Index 144

Foreword **Luiz Camillo Osorio**

During a visit to the Museu de Arte Moderna do Rio de Janeiro in late 2009, Mark Wigley (Dean of Columbia University's Graduate School of Architecture) made a categorical remark: "If I had to save a few late twentieth century buildings from an atomic explosion, this museum by Affonso Eduardo Reidy would surely be among them." In so doing, he confirmed the need for a book edited by the museum and focused on such a project. Additionally, from the moment I took on curatorship of the MAM, I intended to pursue connections for a series of publications.

Rodrigo Fiães' personal commitment and Armínio Fraga's embrace of the project were key in obtaining Gávea Investimentos' support of the MAM and of this publication. Next, we sought out Cobogó publishers whose editors Isabel Diegues and Ricardo Sardenberg were soon on board with the idea and the partnership. It was our intention to produce a book that would at once target specialist readers and laypersons interested in art and architecture. Ana Luiza Nobre was commissioned to write a critical essay that would account for Reidy's place and that of the MAM project within the history of modern Brazilian architecture and Rio's urban development. The architect's characteristically sharp and precise lines envision architecture within the broader context of the city, reconfiguring and refunctionalizing its spaces. In addition to the critical text, the book includes highly generous words by Paulo Mendes da Rocha especially written for this publication. As noted in his text: "As a building, the MAM is irreplaceable in the education of Brazilian architects and its stimulating creative and constructivist power has marked São Paulo architecture and influenced all subsequent generations. What is known as 'our architecture' would be inconceivable without the vivid presence of this architect from Rio de Janeiro." The principal architect of his generation recognizes Reidy's determining influence upon contemporary architecture and, especially, upon the São Paulo school.

Given how fully it allows us to understand the project's complexity and elegance, the Memorial introducing MAM and written by Reidy himself is a fundamental part of this book. The conceptual and spatial articulation of the School, the Exhibition and the Theater buildings speaks for itself. A photographic essay by Vicente de Mello completes the book. Beyond the fact that he is one of our most important contemporary photographers, his intimate experience of its spaces over the years in which he worked at the museum are embedded in his body and his gaze. Image research was overseen by the MAM center for documentation. Frederico Coelho (my curatorial assistant) was instrumental in articulating the research and editing the material.

For a curator, working in this space is both a privilege and an enormous challenge. The Monumental Room is a large space – public in scale – that calls for powerful works to support it and the force of its huge back wall. The large second floor gallery has windows run along the full length of its 2000 column-free square meters and is a versatile area in which wide spaces and intimate rooms alike may be created. It is our hope that the present volume will come to play a critical part in architectural studies, thus contributing to a growing appreciation for our city as the first in a series of publications on the museum and Brazilian art to be produced by MAM itself.

Luiz Camillo Osorio
Curator
Museu de Arte Moderna do Rio de Janeiro

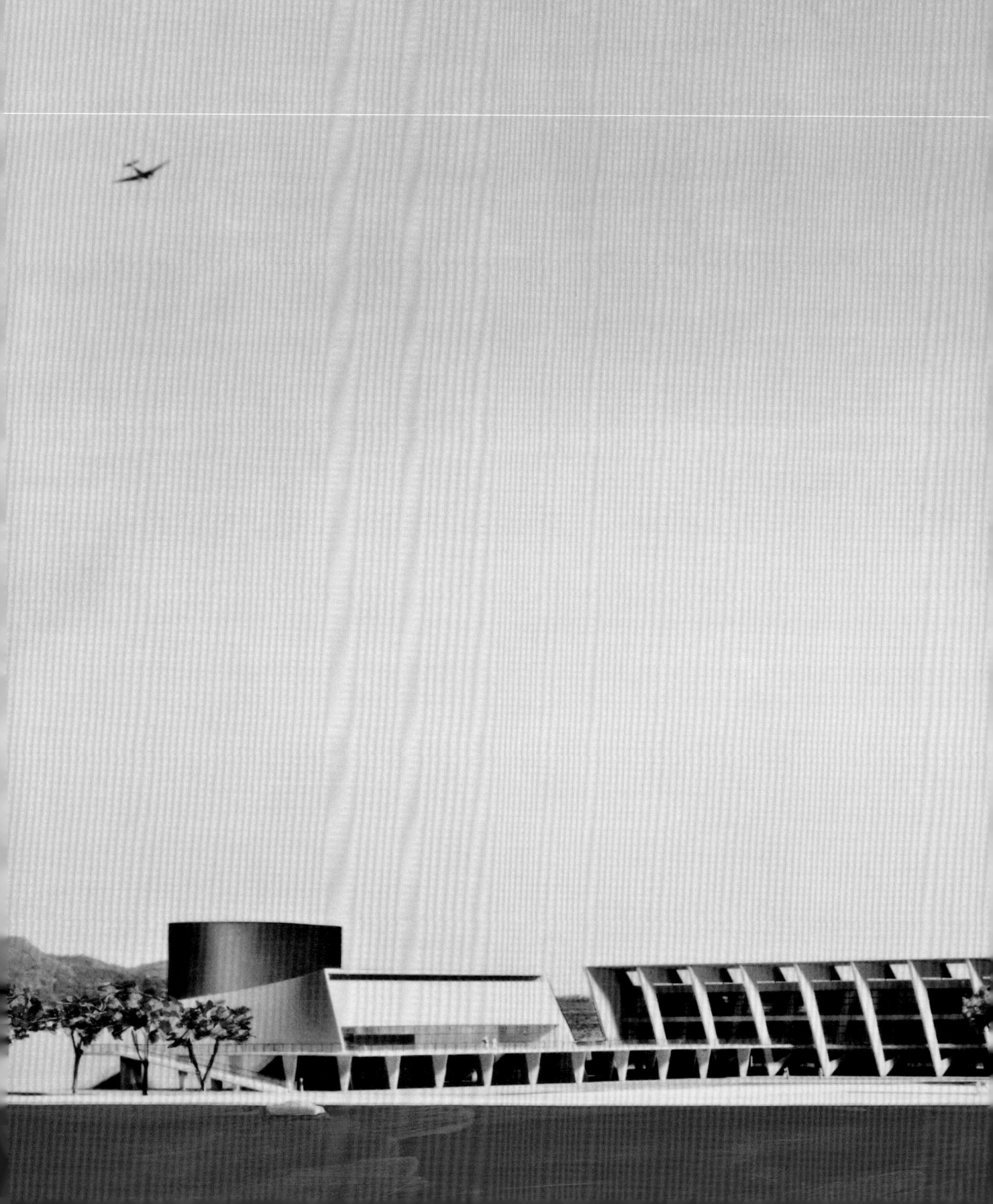

Descriptive Memorial **Affonso Eduardo Reidy**

If the correspondence between an architectural work and the physical environment that surrounds it is always a matter of gravest importance, in the case of the Museu de Arte Moderna do Rio de Janeiro building this condition takes on even greater consequence, given the privileged location in which it is being constructed – within the very heart of the city, in the midst of a vast area that is soon to be a beautiful public park overlooking the sea and facing the entrance to the bar and encircled by the world's most beautiful landscape. As much as possible, it was the architect's ongoing concern to prevent the building from becoming an element that would disturb the landscape or clash with nature. Hence the decision to adopt predominantly horizontal lines counterposed to the busy outline of the mountain range and the employment of a thoroughly pierced, transparent structure that would allow its gardens to continue through the building itself all the way to the sea, leaving a considerable part of the ground floor free. Rather than confine the art works between four walls, totally isolated from the world outside, an open solution was adopted in which the nature around it might participate in the spectacle offered to the museum visitor.

The traditional concept of a museum has undergone a great many changes over the past forty years. It ceased to be a passive organism and took on an important educational function and a high social meaning, rendering knowledge and understanding of the most striking manifestations of world artistic creation accessible to the public and providing adequate training to a contingent of artists who are perfectly attuned to the spirit of their time, all of them potential influences upon standards of quality in industrial production.

Yet it was not only the concept of museums that was transformed: the very notion of architectural space has been modified. The development of new construction techniques has paved the way for the "independent structure" and, consequently, to the "open floor plan" – this is to say that function is therefore performed now exclusively by columns; freed from their former structural responsibility they have therefore – and with hitherto unimaginable freedom – come to play the role of simple screening elements; freely arranged lightweight panels made of various materials offering the widest possible range of spatial organization. Thus a new concept of architectural space emerges – channeled "fluid space" has replaced the outdated notion of "confined space" within the boundaries of a cubic compartment.

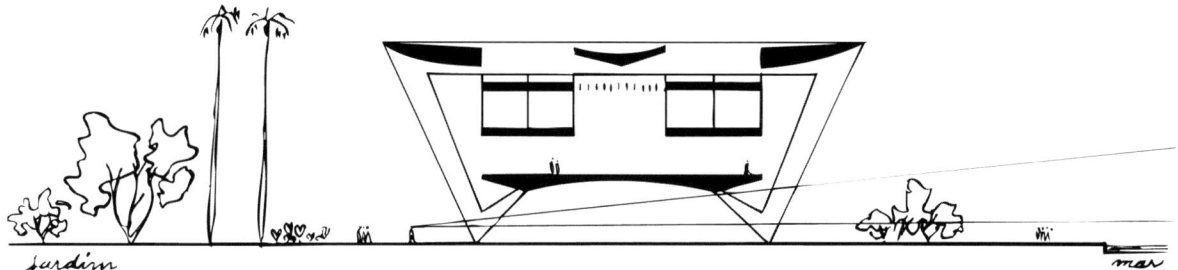

Encompassing all the contemporary manifestations of the visual arts, the Museu de Arte Moderna do Rio de Janeiro's eminently dynamic action requires an architectural structure that will provide it with maximum flexibility in the use of its spaces, allowing for the use of large areas as well as the setting up of small rooms in which given works may be contemplated in more intimate settings. The Rio de Janeiro's MAM exhibition gallery was designed with this objective: it occupies an area 130 meters long by 26 meters wide that is entirely free of columns so as to offer absolute freedom in the setting up of exhibitions. This area will have a variable height: part of it will be 8 meters high, part of it 6.40 meters and the remainder 3.60 meters high.

Natural light imparts a sense of life and movement to these spaces, enhancing the works on exhibition through the variety of sensations provided by daylight. At its zenith, light is diffuse and uniform; there are no shadows, there is no relief, the environment becomes neutral and inexpressive. When it comes from the side, directing space and providing objects with relief, it further provides visitors with the possibility of visual contact with the exterior. Nevertheless, a rigid and exclusive system would limit the freedom of showing under the most favorable conditions works that might occasionally be enhanced by overhead or even artificial lighting. Those parts of the MAM exhibition gallery with the lowest ceiling height will be sidelit and in those parts with a double ceiling height through sheds and clerestories.

Generally speaking, the fact that natural light presents more advantages than artificial light for the presentation of works does not diminish the importance of that which the latter represents to the Museum now a days. Artificial lighting is obviously indispensable, not only for evening, but for the exhibition of objects that might be harmed by sunlight such as drawings, fabric, etc. The quality of light to be employed is another point of importance in an art museum. Incandescent light is rich in red and orange rays that modify the aspect of certain colors. In turn, fluorescent light imparts a sensation of coldness and likewise alters the aspect of colors. However, combination of the two will allow a closer resemblance to the effect of sunlight. A very flexible system has been projected for the MAM: the exhibition gallery ceiling will be garnished with clear sheets of plastic vinyl that will diffuse the light emitted by fluorescent tubes, providing the environment with soft lighting. The luminous surface will thus be interrupted every two meters by reflectors of incandescent set in transversal slits and equipped with the appropriate lenses, directed precisely to those spots that need to be lit, without producing reflections or blinding the visitors. The whole of the building's second floor will be used for exhibitions and the third floor will be partially occupied by a 200 seat auditorium with equipment for film projection, a film library, a library, the museum's board offices, administrative services and a storeroom for works not on exhibition. This storeroom, in which works shall be kept in perfect safety, will be temperature and humidity-controlled and will be completely isolated from the atmospheric variations of the exterior. Canvases will be fixed on lightweight runners set at a small distance from one another, thus allowing storage of large numbers of canvases within a small space while ensuring perfect climate conditions and easy examination by interested parties.

The museum's auxiliary services and installations will occupy part of the building's ground floor and basement, including the service entrance and locations for the unpacking, identification and registration of works, deposits, workshops and laboratories, the print room and a large room for preparing exhibitions. The ground floor will also house the Technical School of Creation. The school's installations will also include spaces for administrative services, several classrooms and studios, a photo lab, typography, bookbinding, a canteen for students, etc. A restaurant and garden terrace that communicate with the exhibition gallery will be located on the second floor of this building.

A one thousand seat theater will be located on the eastern extremity of this complex. Its stage will be 50 meters wide, 20 meters deep and have 20 meters of free space between the stage and the fly system. The stage is complemented by an electronically-activated system of vagons that may be moved into the lateral wings and upstage. The front of the stage will be 7,50 meters high and 12 meters wide, although the side panels may open to a full width of 16 meters for symphony concerts.

Affonso Eduardo Reidy
Architect, 1953

About the Memorial

This descriptive memorial was written in 1953 by architect Affonso Eduardo Reidy shortly before construction work began on the magnificent Museu de Arte Moderna do Rio de Janeiro. The degree to which he described his project reflects the care with which he conceived and elaborated it. Actual construction began in 1954 and ended (on at least two of its buildings) in 1967, having remained under the architect's supervision until his untimely death in 1967.

Since then, over four decades separate the MAM of today from the MAM proposed in Reidy's text. Should an architect or ordinary visitor seek to locate all of the elements described therein, he would most assuredly not find exactly what was planned. In spite of the fact that it basically held to the original project's principal directives and ideas, the passage of time has led the museum to adapt to changes and events that have taken place throughout the history of its architecture and of the institution itself. For instance, although the Theater was part of the original project it was not completed until 2006, with but a few alterations to the originally-proposed dimensions. Another change in the museum's spatial organization lies in the location of the library and film theater that are a fundamental part of the museum's history. As Reidy points out in his memorial, until the 1970s the museum library and its film theater were located on the third floor of the Exhibition Block. Today, while the library is located within the School Block, and connected to the museum's center for documentation and research, the auditorium and film library are located on the ground floor, as an extension of the same block. One of the museum's technical departments occupies the former auditorium and original library.

With regard to the interior aspects of the Exhibition Block, its artificial lighting and the blinds that were once part of the rooms were destroyed in the fire that ravaged the museum in July of 1978. In spite of the fact that the museum's external structure remained intact after the fire, new air conditioning and lighting systems needed to be adapted to other technologies, with minimal changes to Reidy's original project. Beyond the modifications that succeeded the accident, the museum's very use by various artists and exhibitions also generated alterations so that the museum could be adapted to new exhibition needs and technologies.

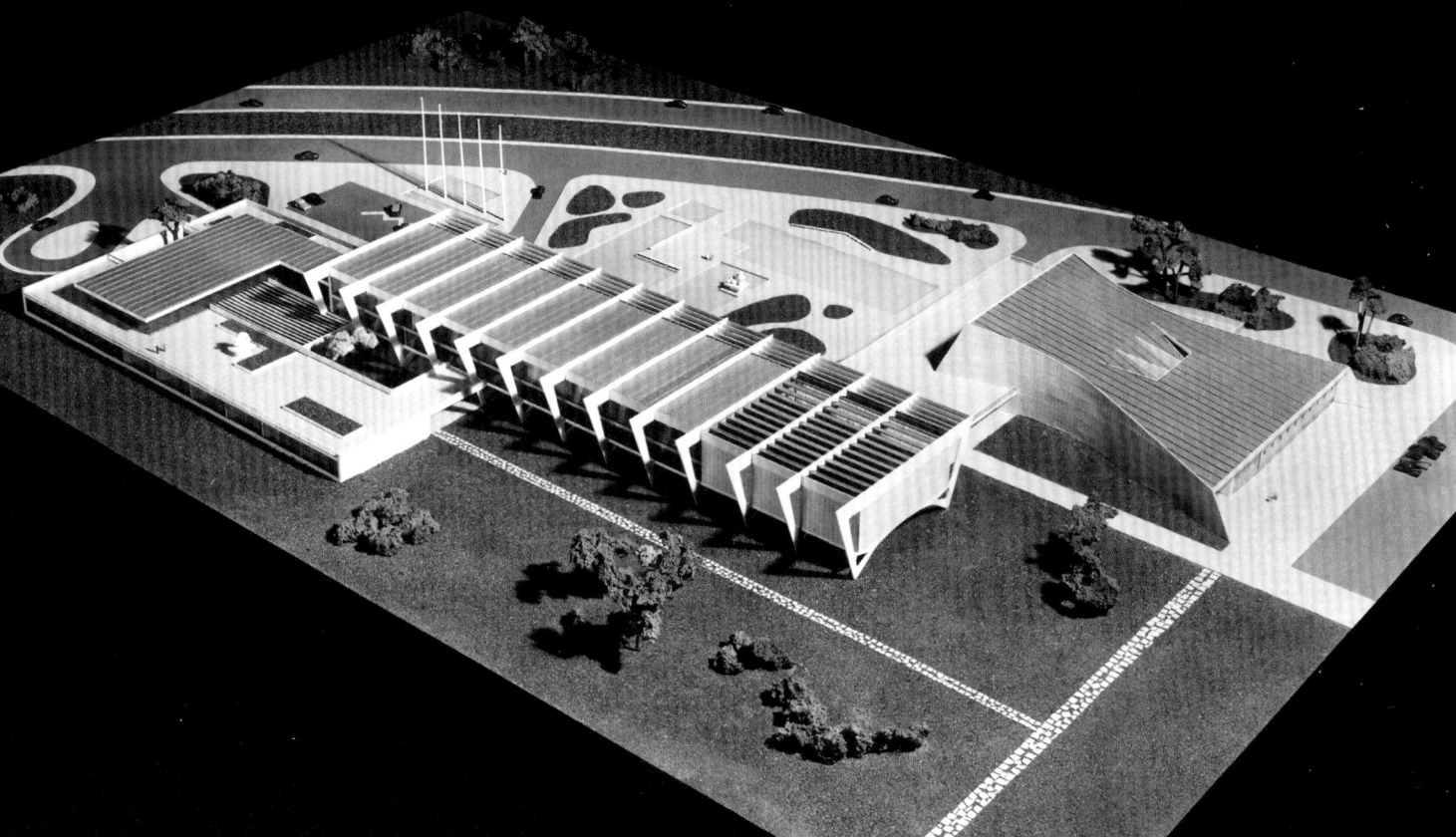

Regardless of such changes and innovations, the Museu de Arte Moderna do Rio de Janeiro remains the faithful portrait of its architect's visionary project, a space whose equilibrium between the concrete lightness of its buildings and the lushness of its natural surroundings continues to impress its visitors to this day. Beyond this, its spatial adaptations to time and contemporary art reflect the way in which the MAM reaffirms its architect's ideals, given that – in his own words – ever since its foundation the museum's calling was to encompass all the visual art forms of our times.

Frederico Coelho
Editor

The Images

Razing, Landfill and Occupation of the Tract

30 Museu de Arte Moderna Rio de Janeiro

Museu de Arte Moderna Rio de Janeiro

Architecture and Construction 33

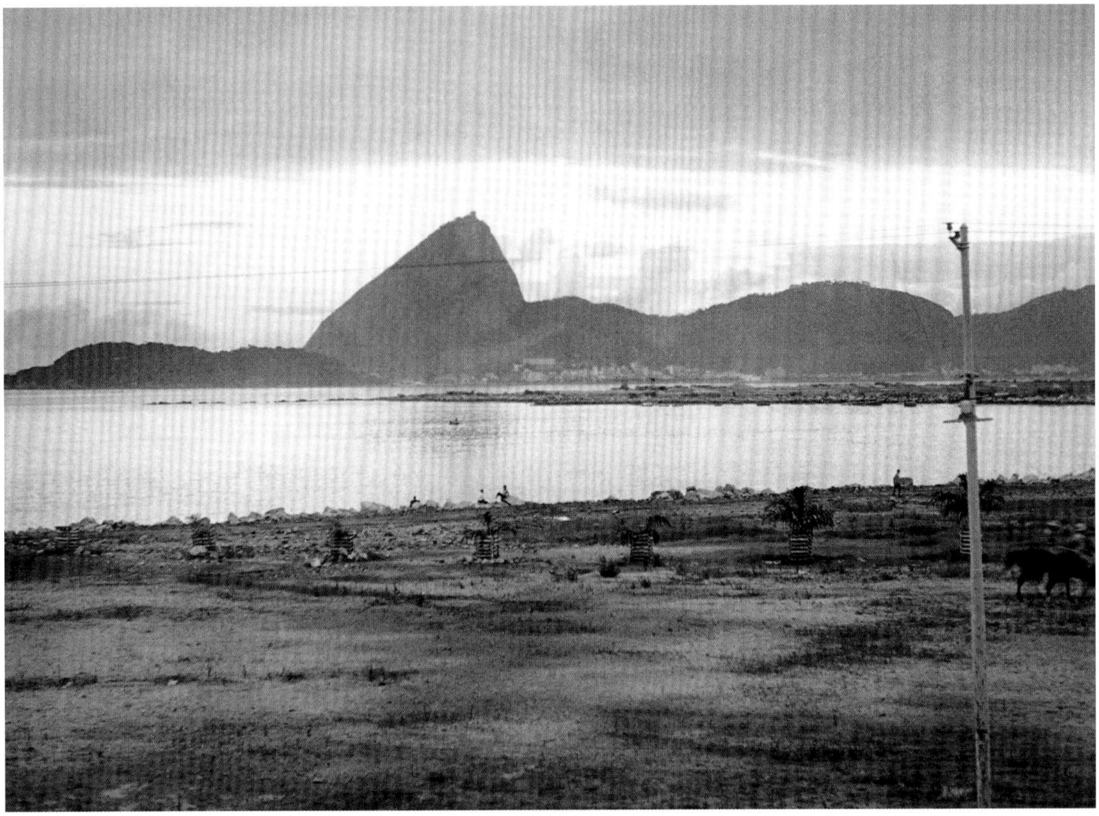

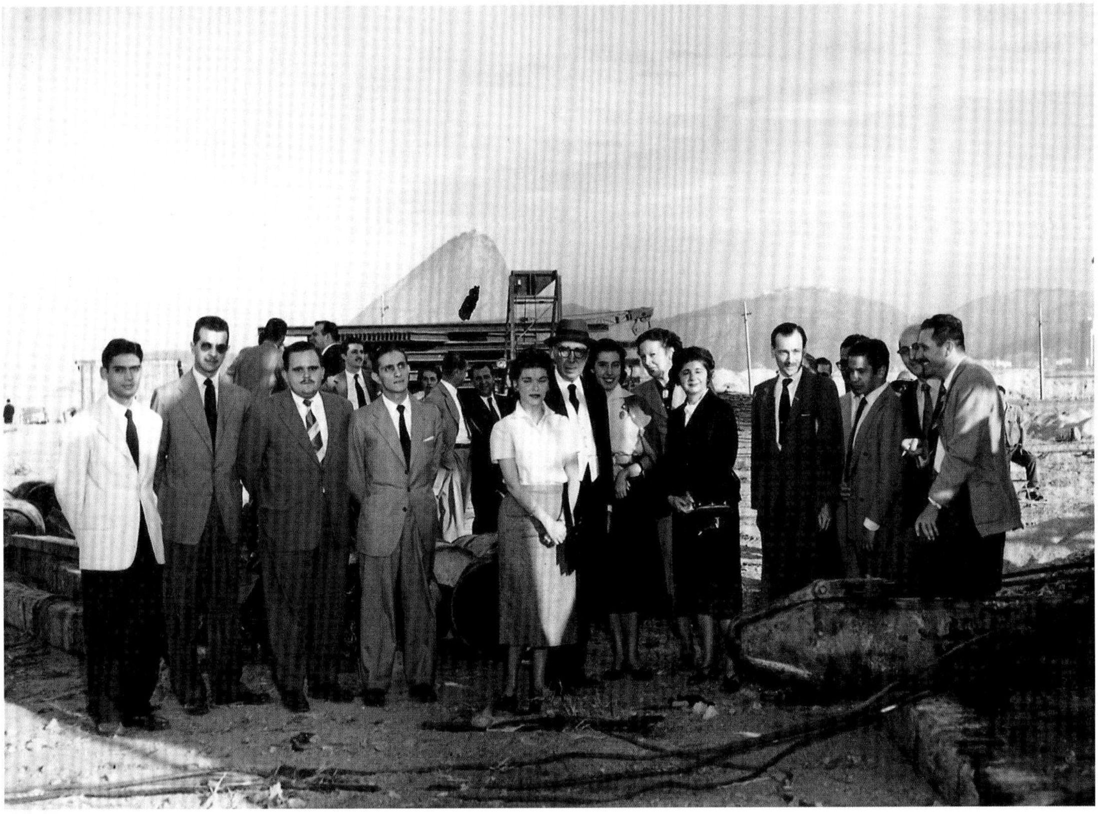

Museu de Arte Moderna Rio de Janeiro

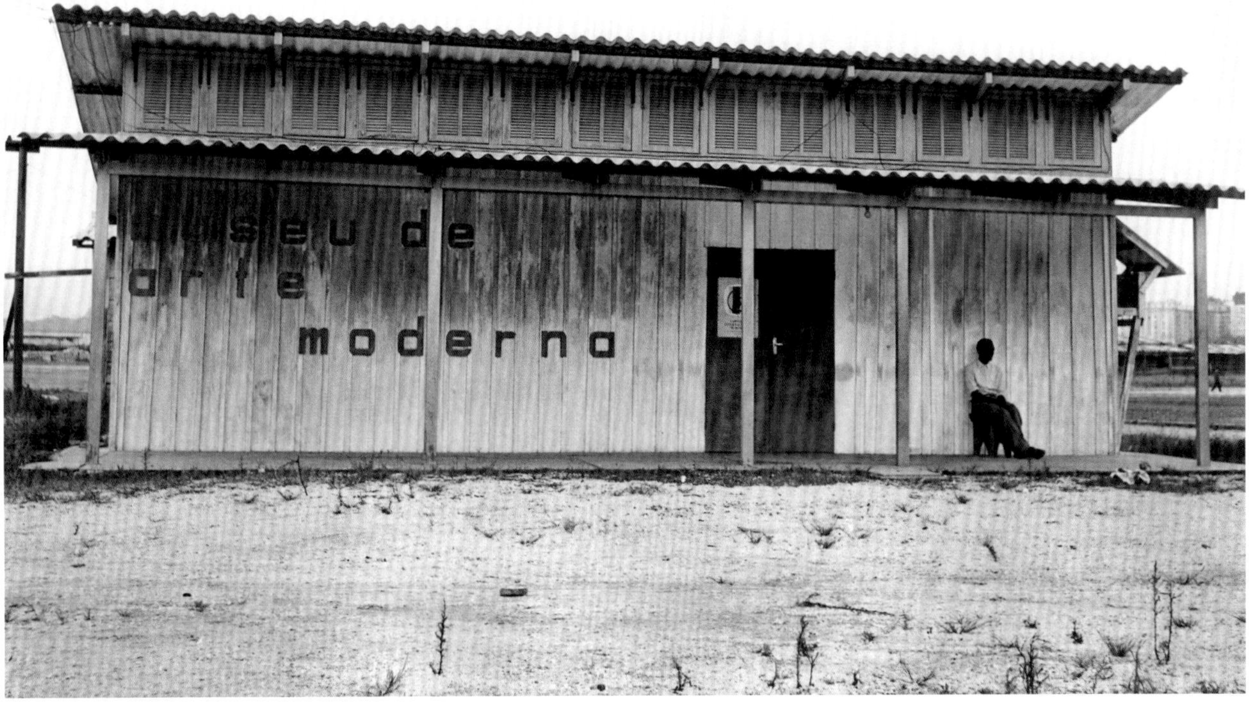
moderna

Preparing for Construction: Piles, Foundations and Structures

Architecture and Construction 41

42 Museu de Arte Moderna Rio de Janeiro

Architecture and Construction   43

44 Museu de Arte Moderna Rio de Janeiro

Architecture and Construction 45

Museu de Arte Moderna Rio de Janeiro

Architecture and Construction 47

Museu de Arte Moderna Rio de Janeiro

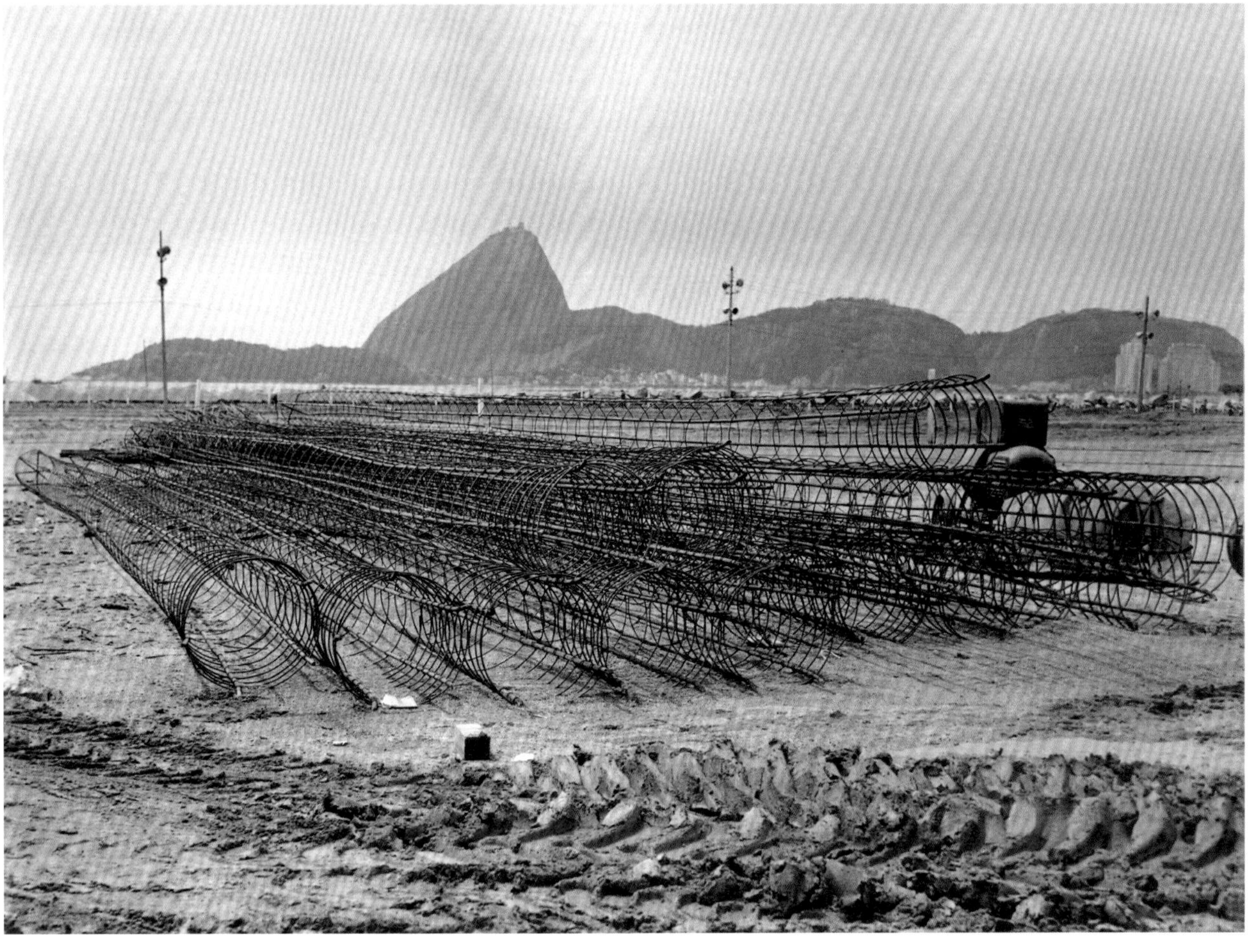

Museu de Arte Moderna Rio de Janeiro

Architecture and Construction 51

Construction of the School Building

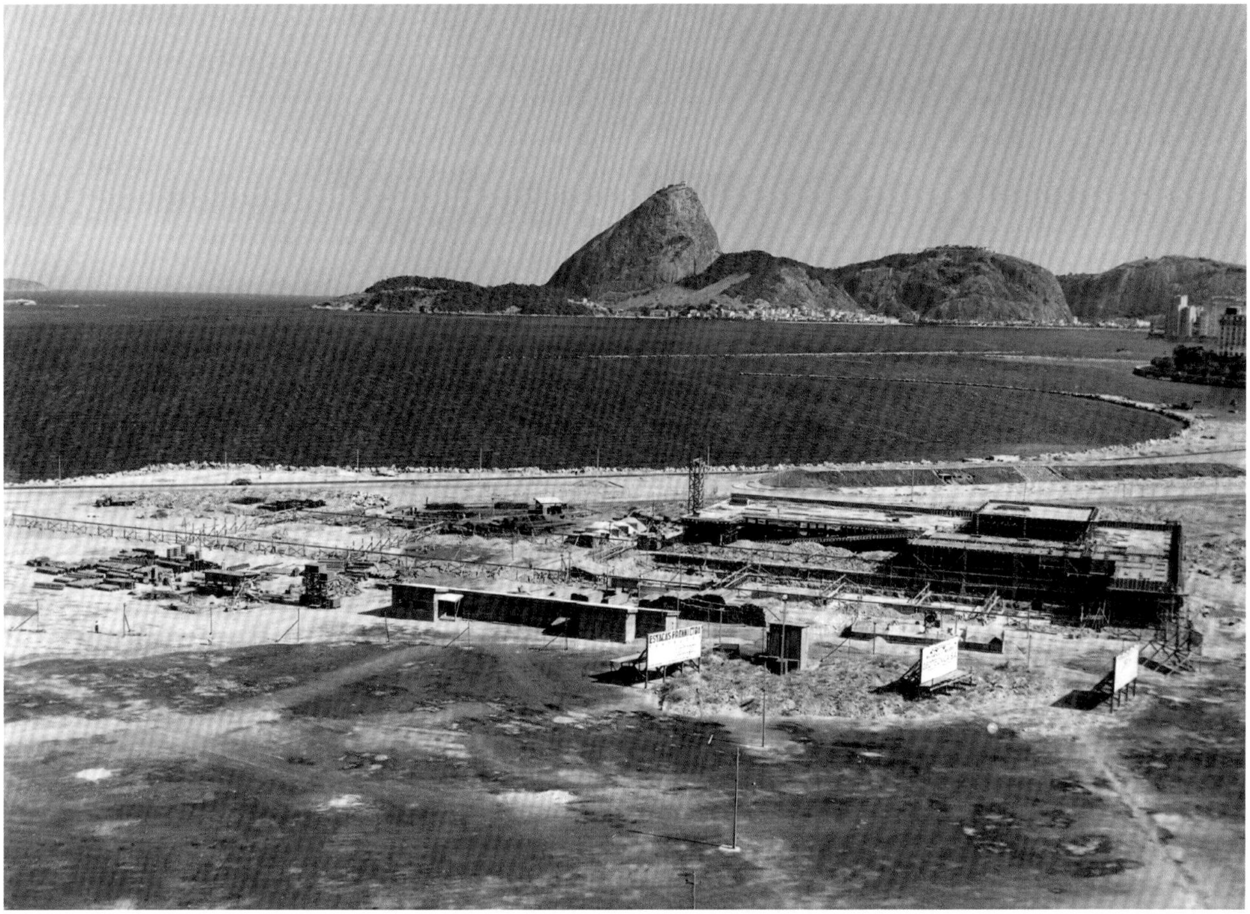

Museu de Arte Moderna Rio de Janeiro

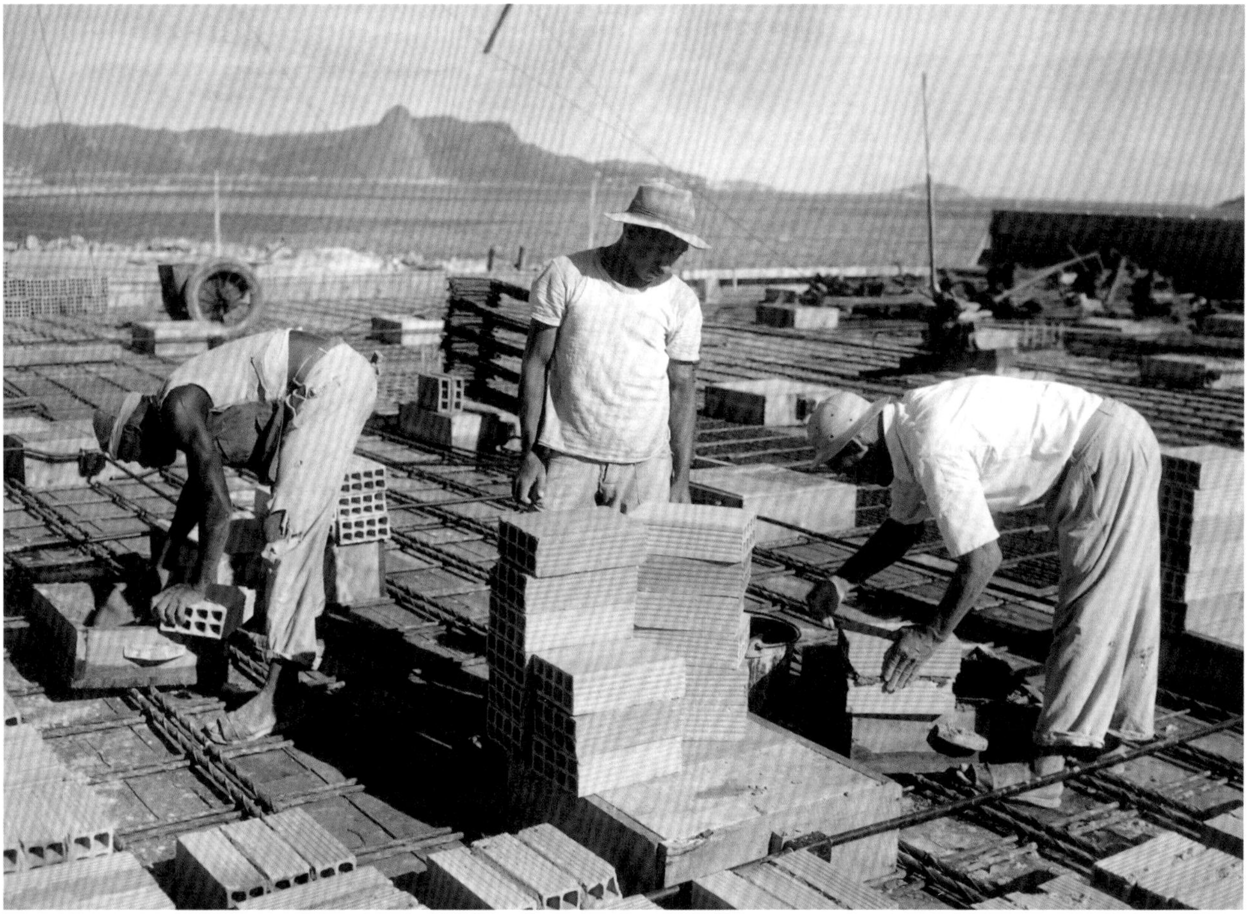

56 Museu de Arte Moderna Rio de Janeiro

Architecture and Construction 57

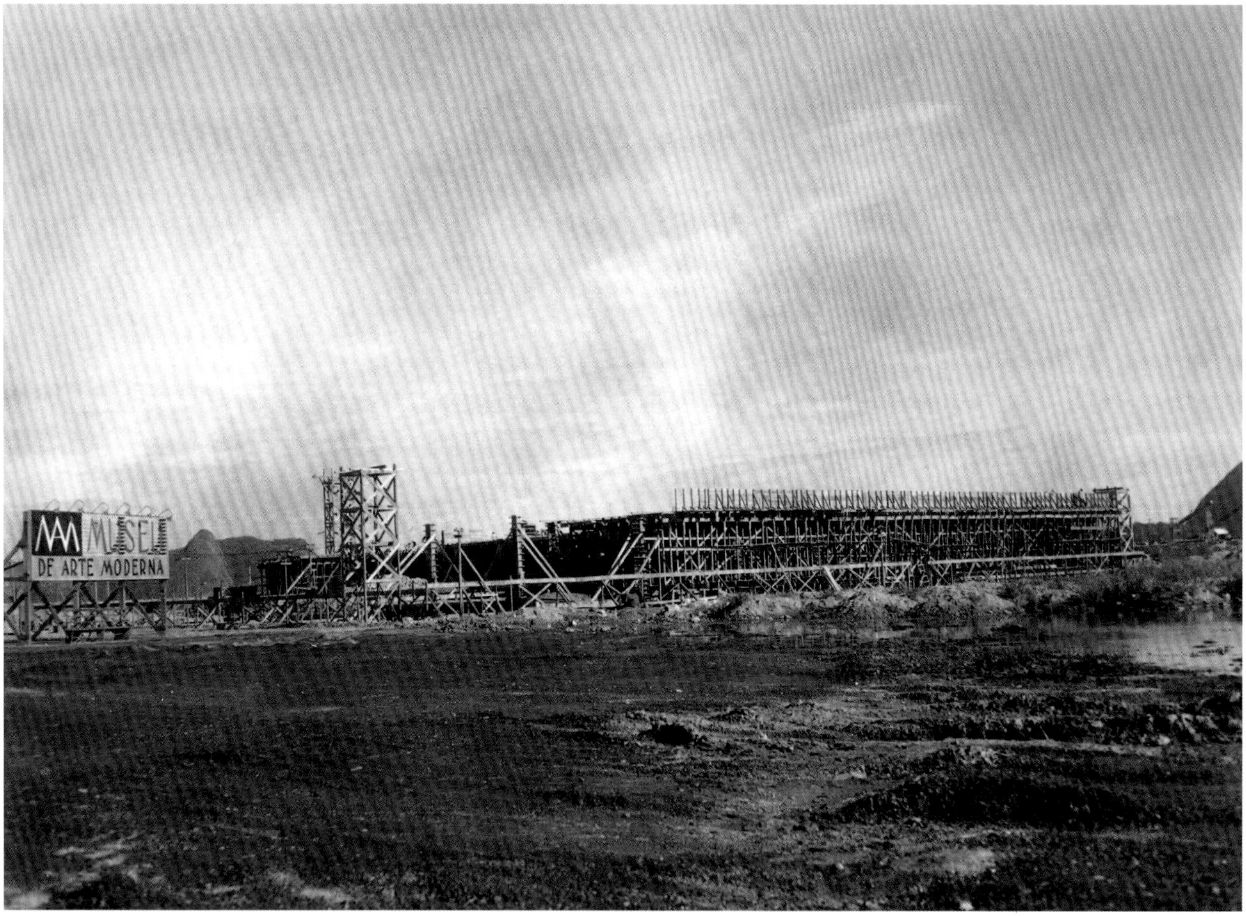
MUSEU
DE ARTE MODERNA

Architecture and Construction   59

Museu de Arte Moderna Rio de Janeiro

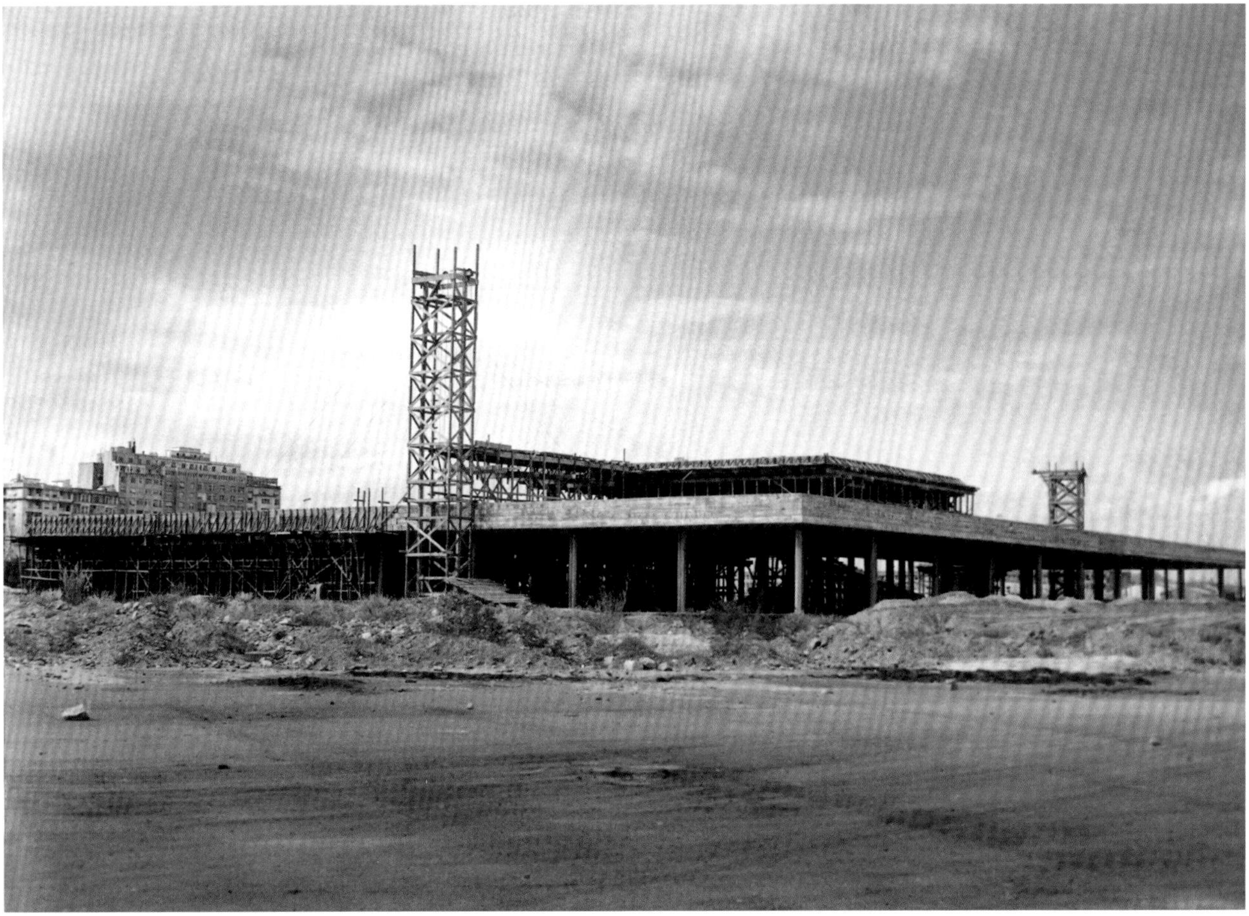

Museu de Arte Moderna Rio de Janeiro

Architecture and Construction 63

Museu de Arte Moderna Rio de Janeiro

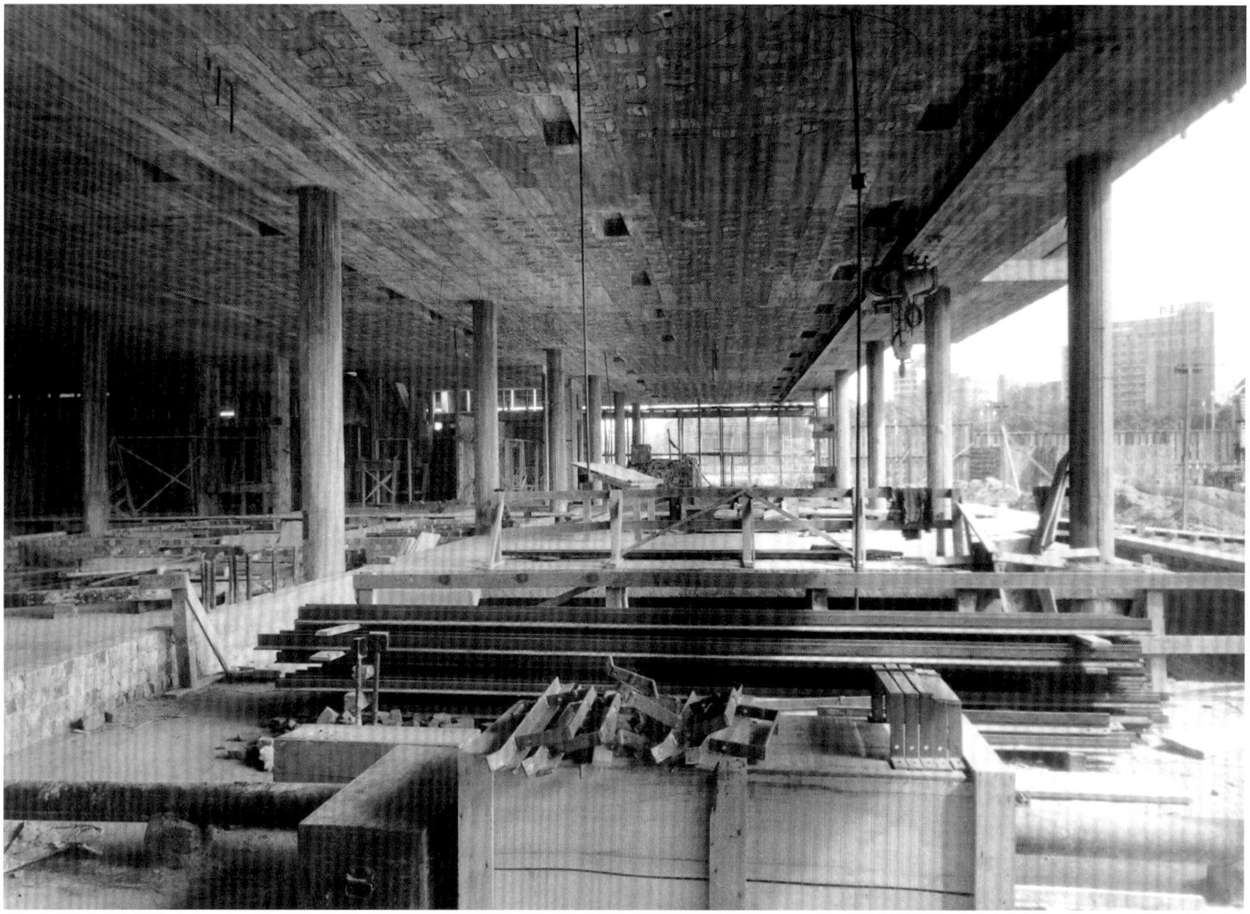

66 Museu de Arte Moderna Rio de Janeiro

Architecture and Construction   67

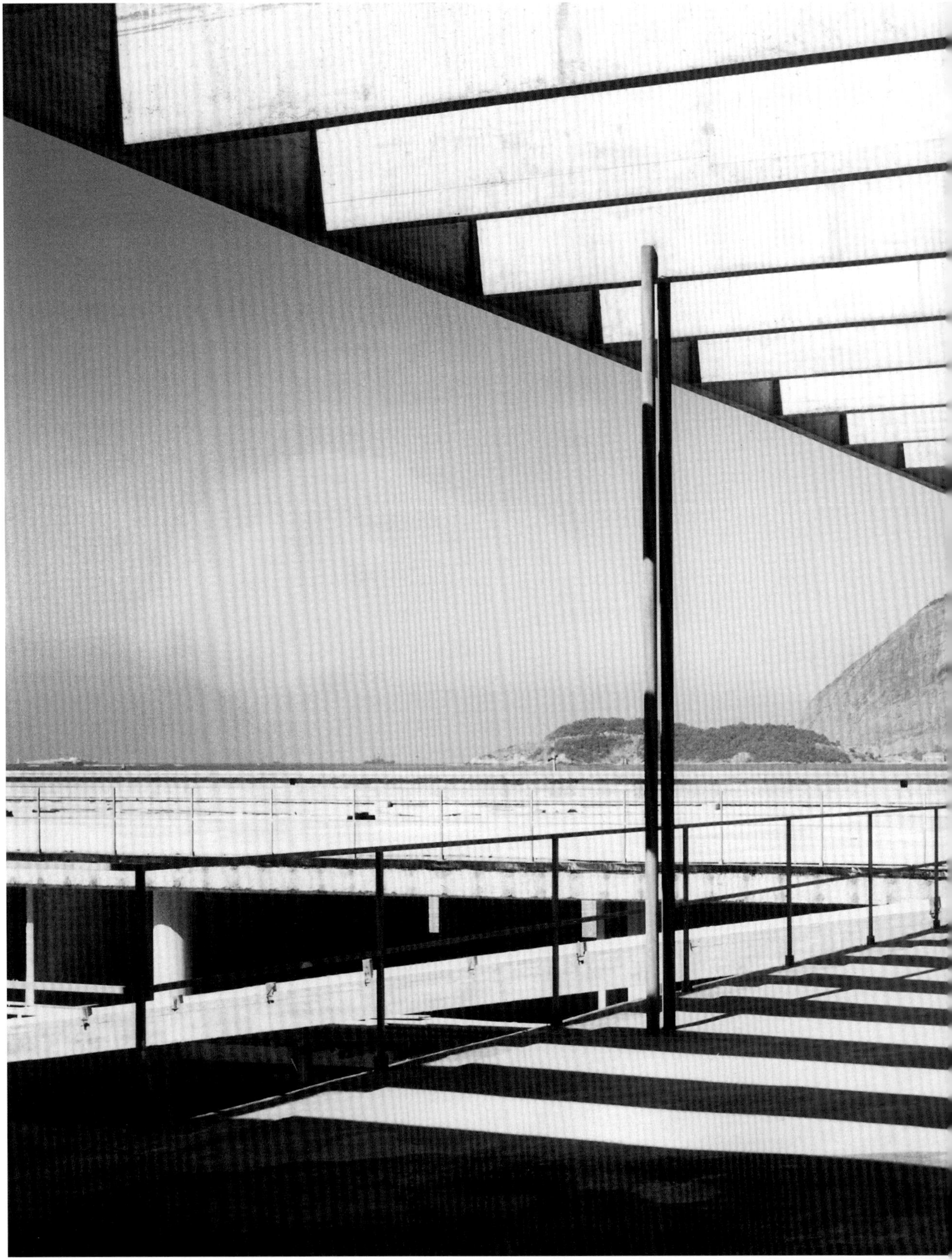

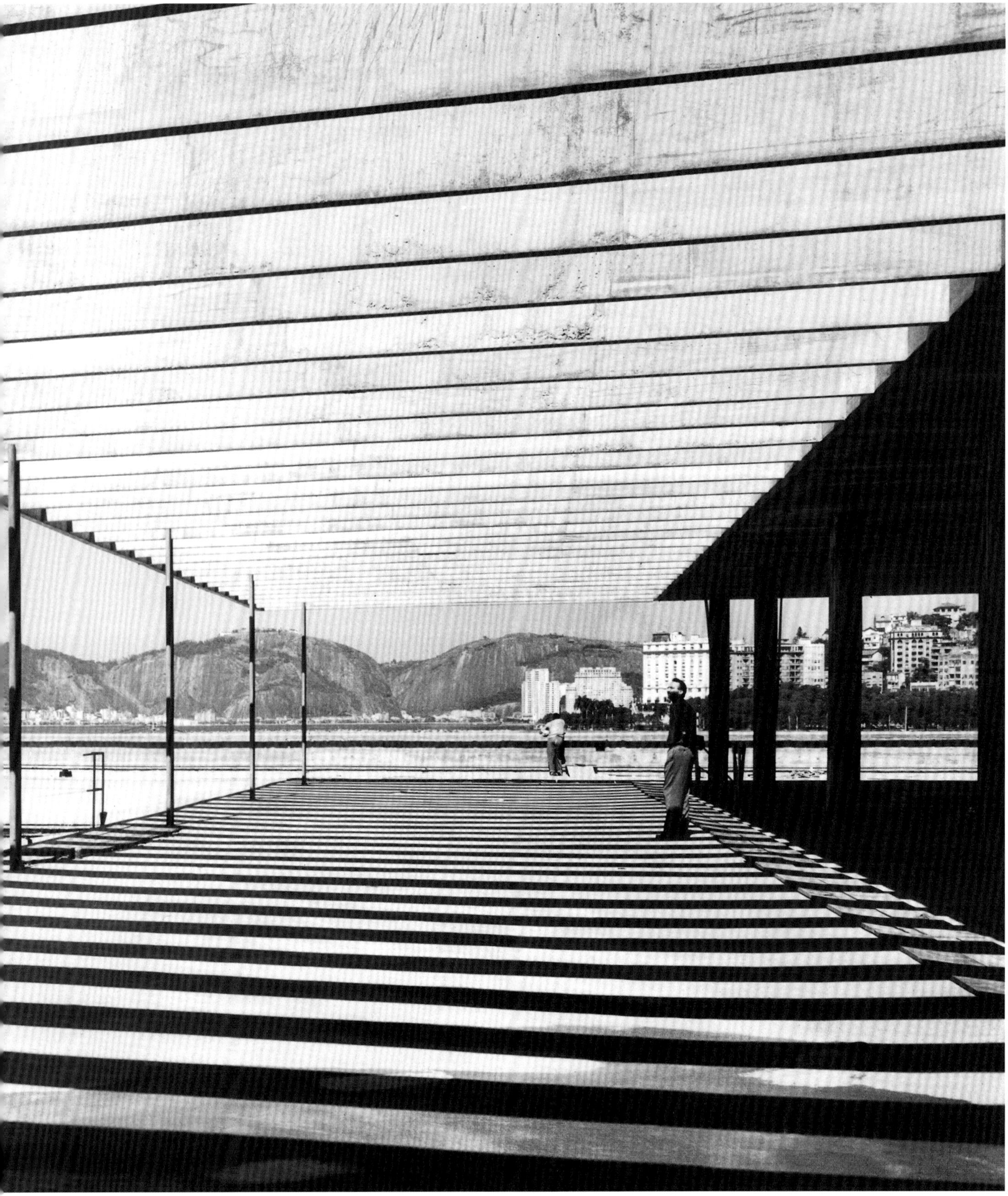

Museu de Arte Moderna Rio de Janeiro

Architecture and Construction 71

Museu de Arte Moderna Rio de Janeiro

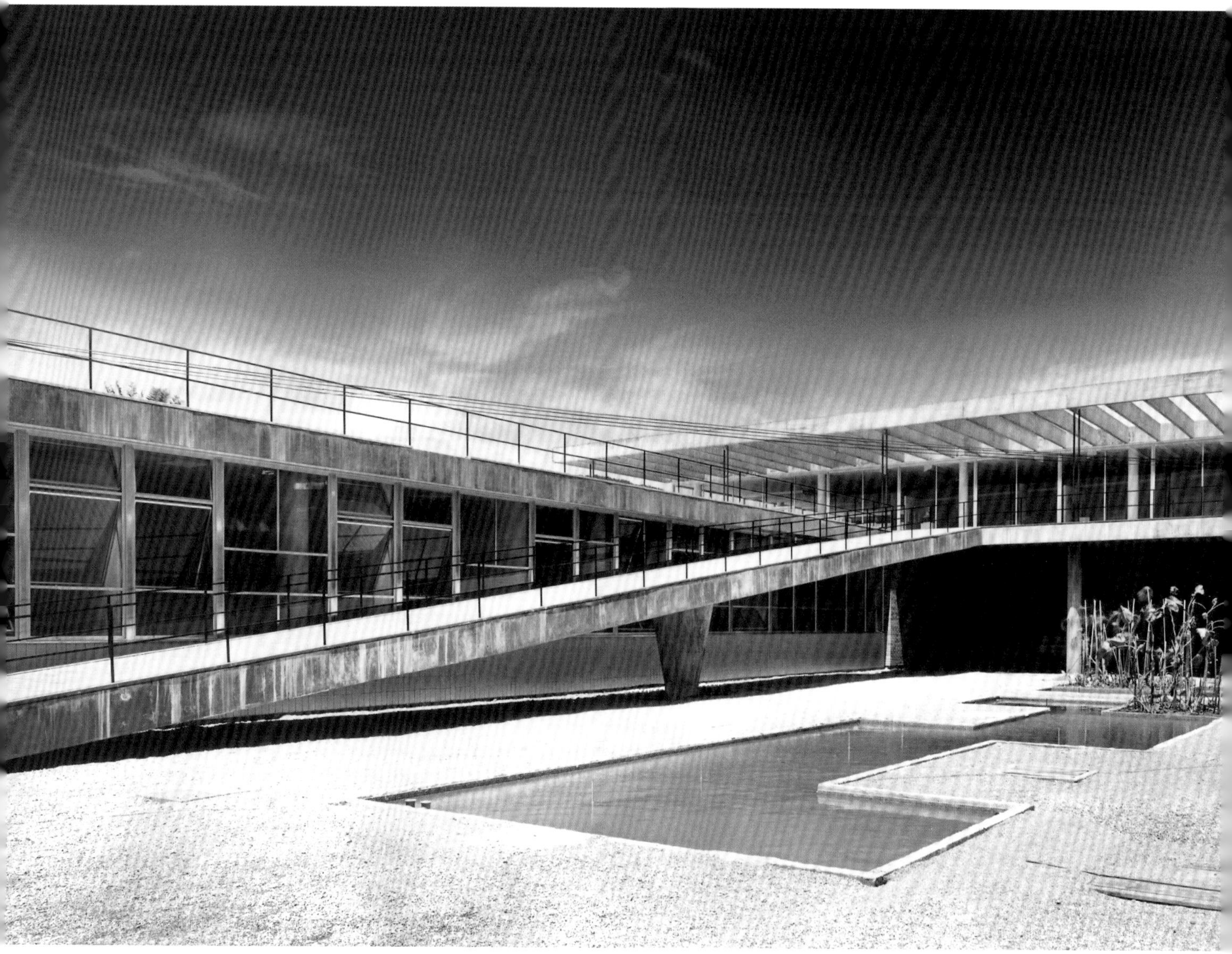

Museu de Arte Moderna Rio de Janeiro

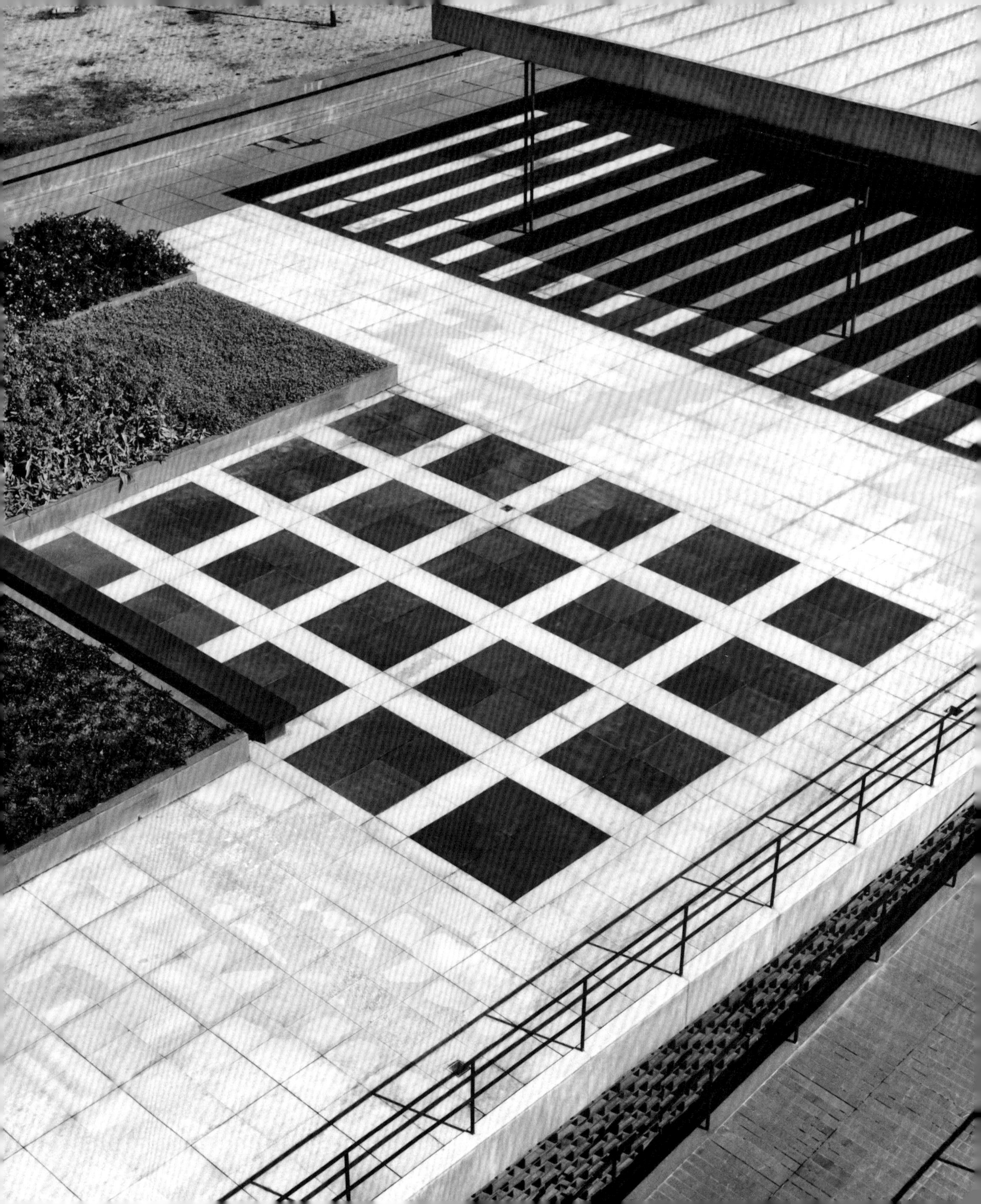

Construction of the Exhibition Building

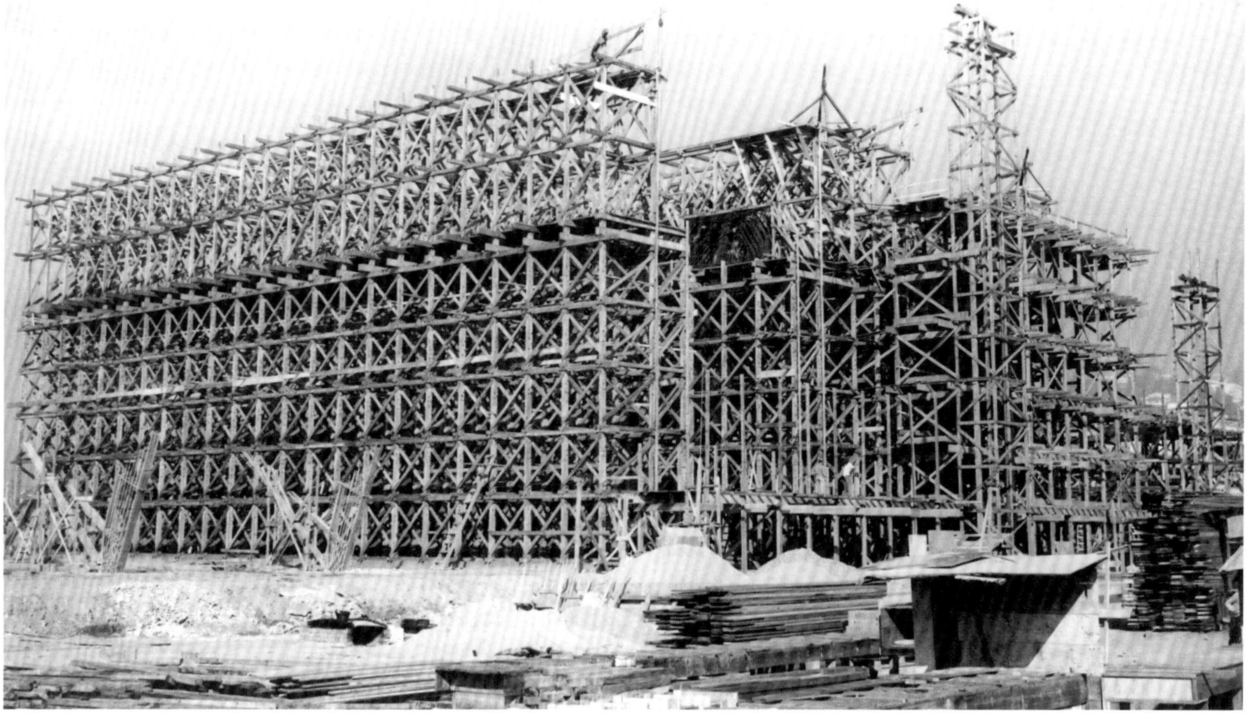

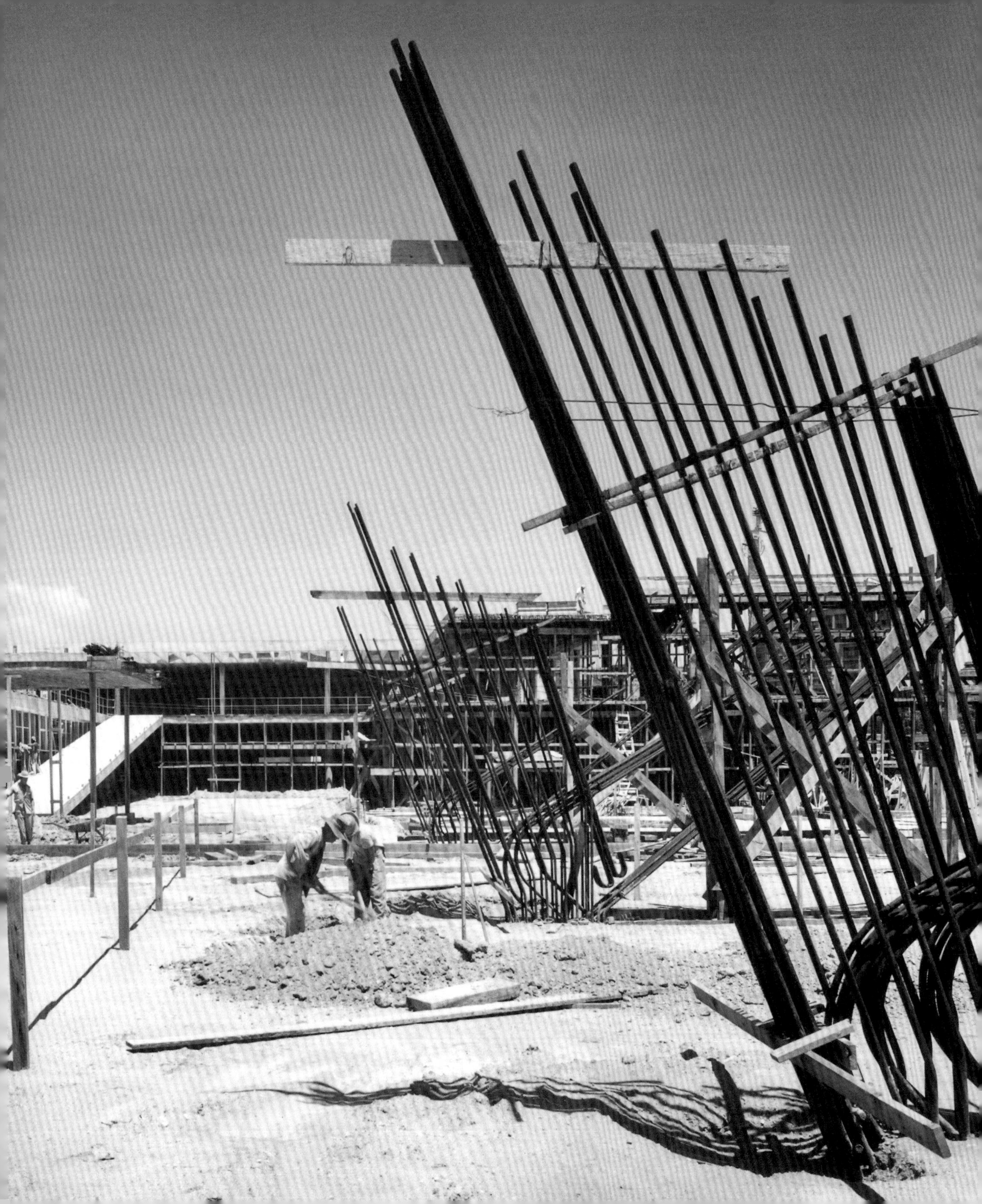

Architecture and Construction 79

Museu de Arte Moderna Rio de Janeiro

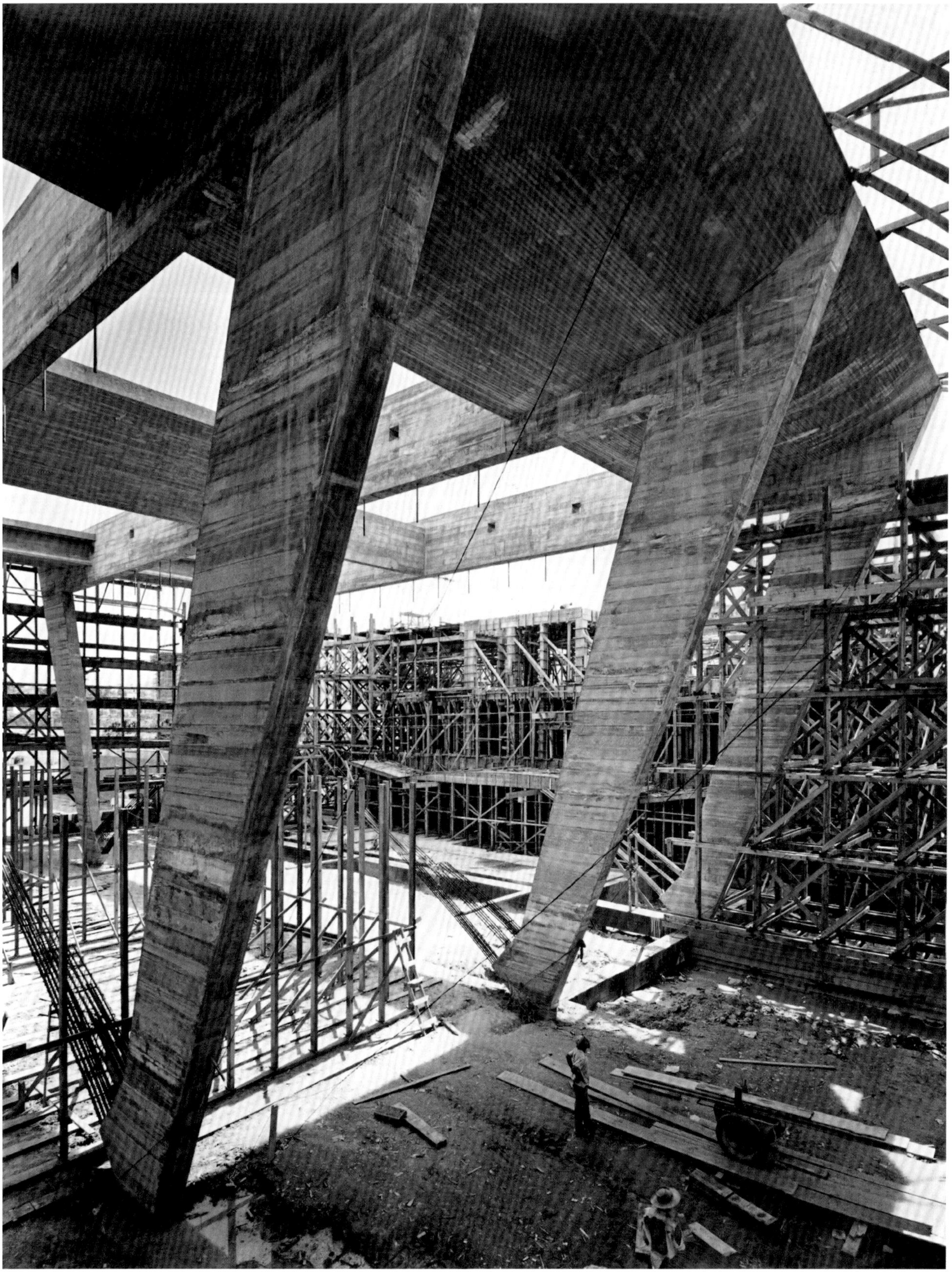

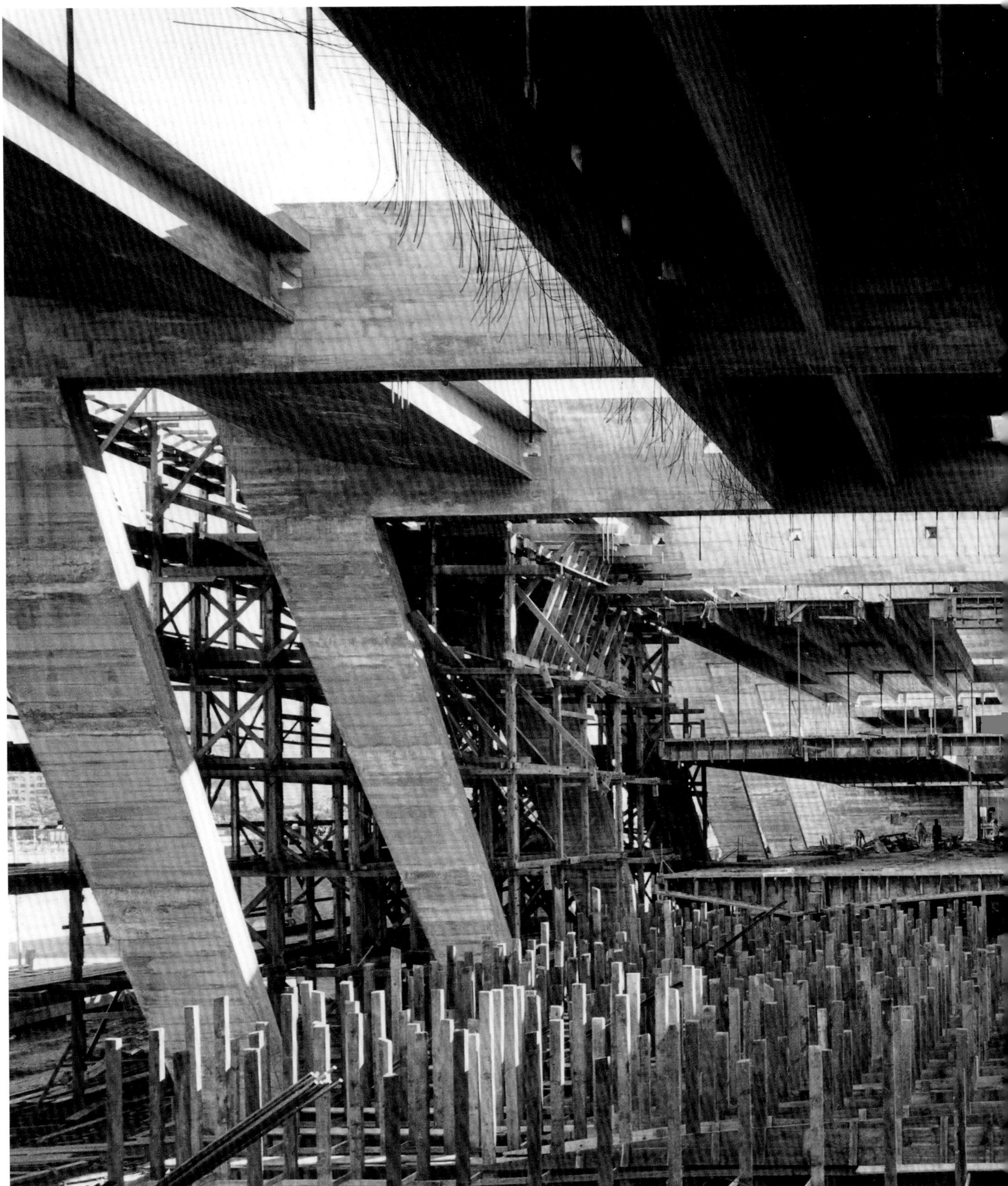

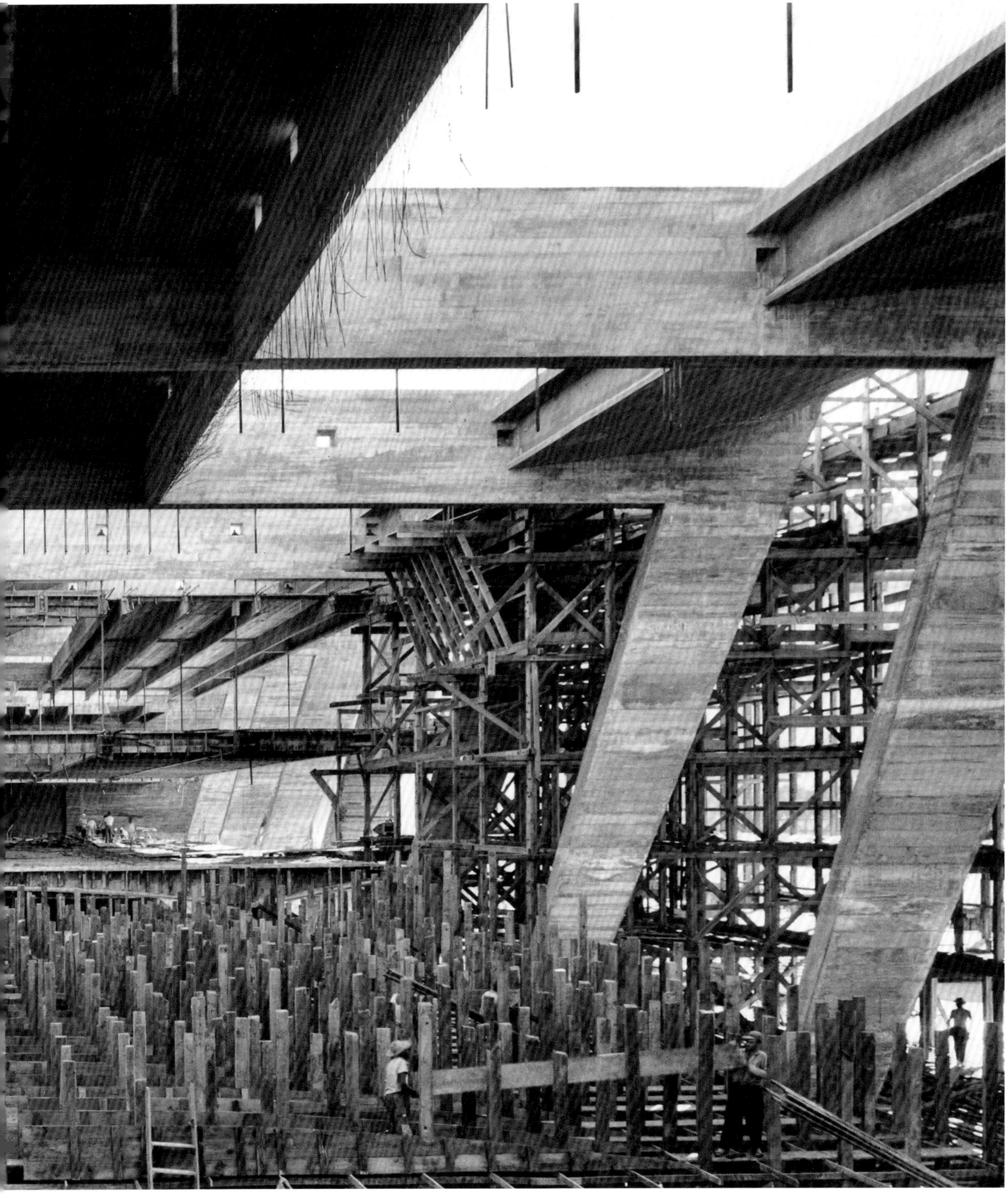

84 Museu de Arte Moderna Rio de Janeiro

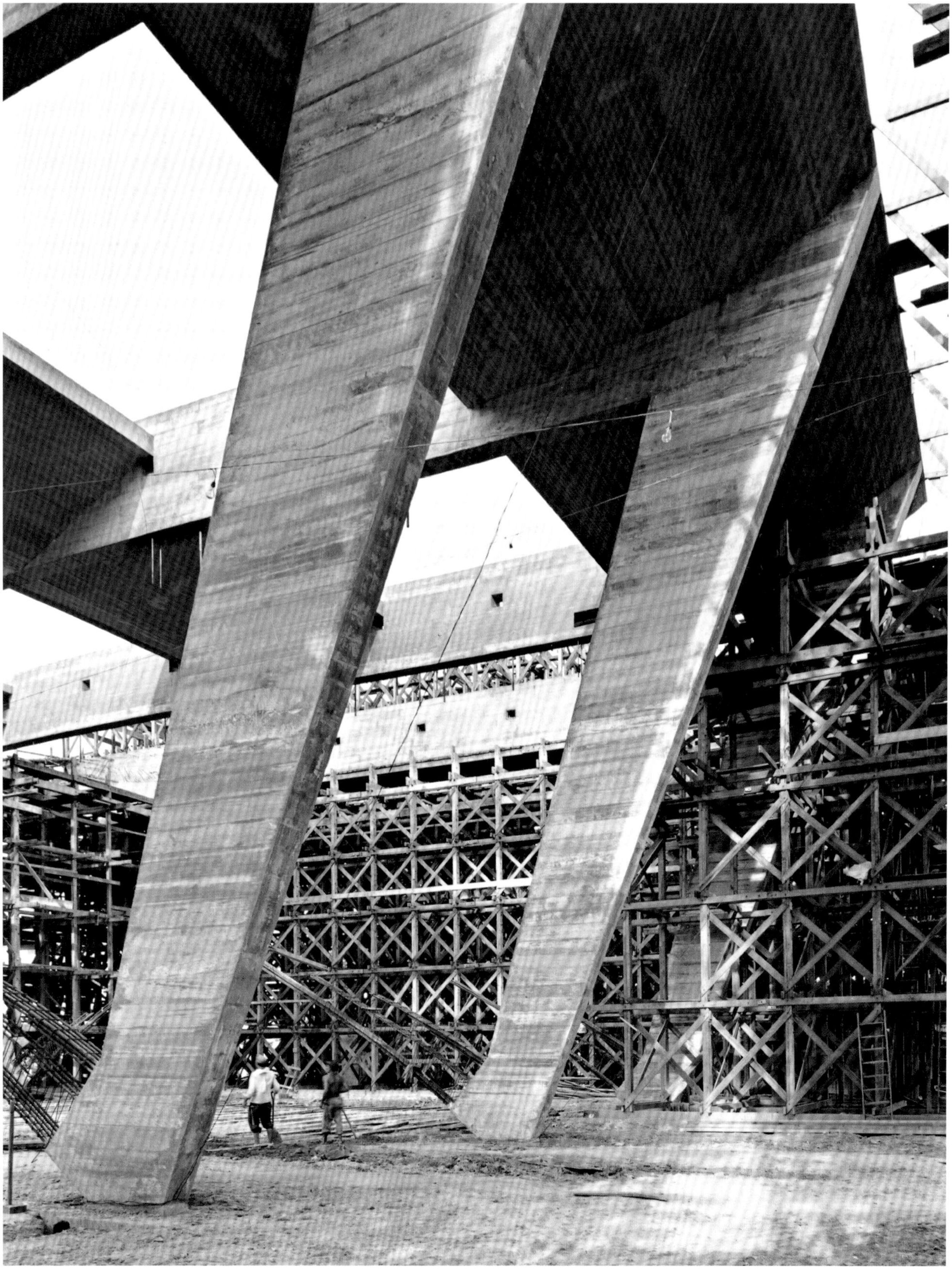

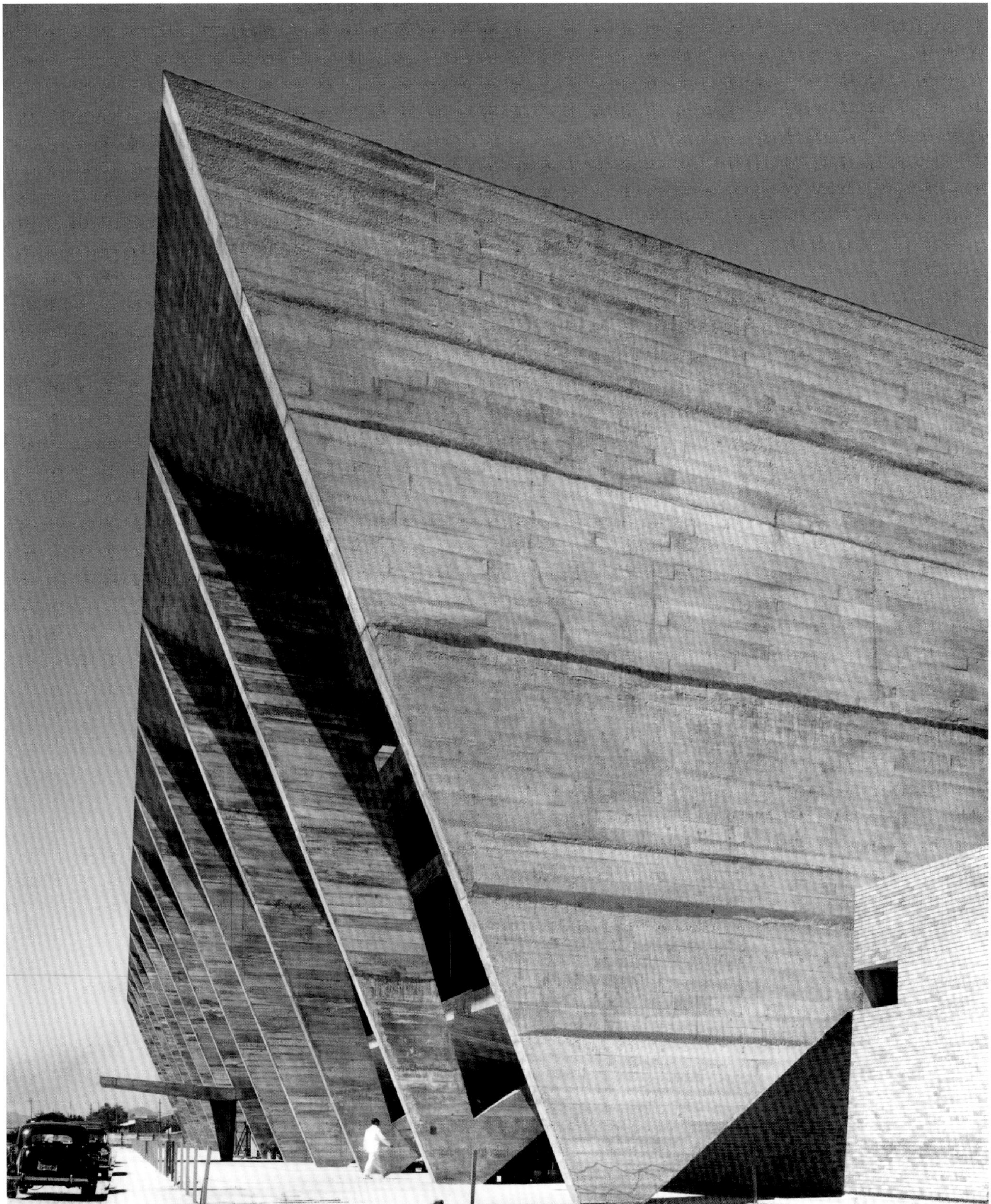

Architecture and Construction   87

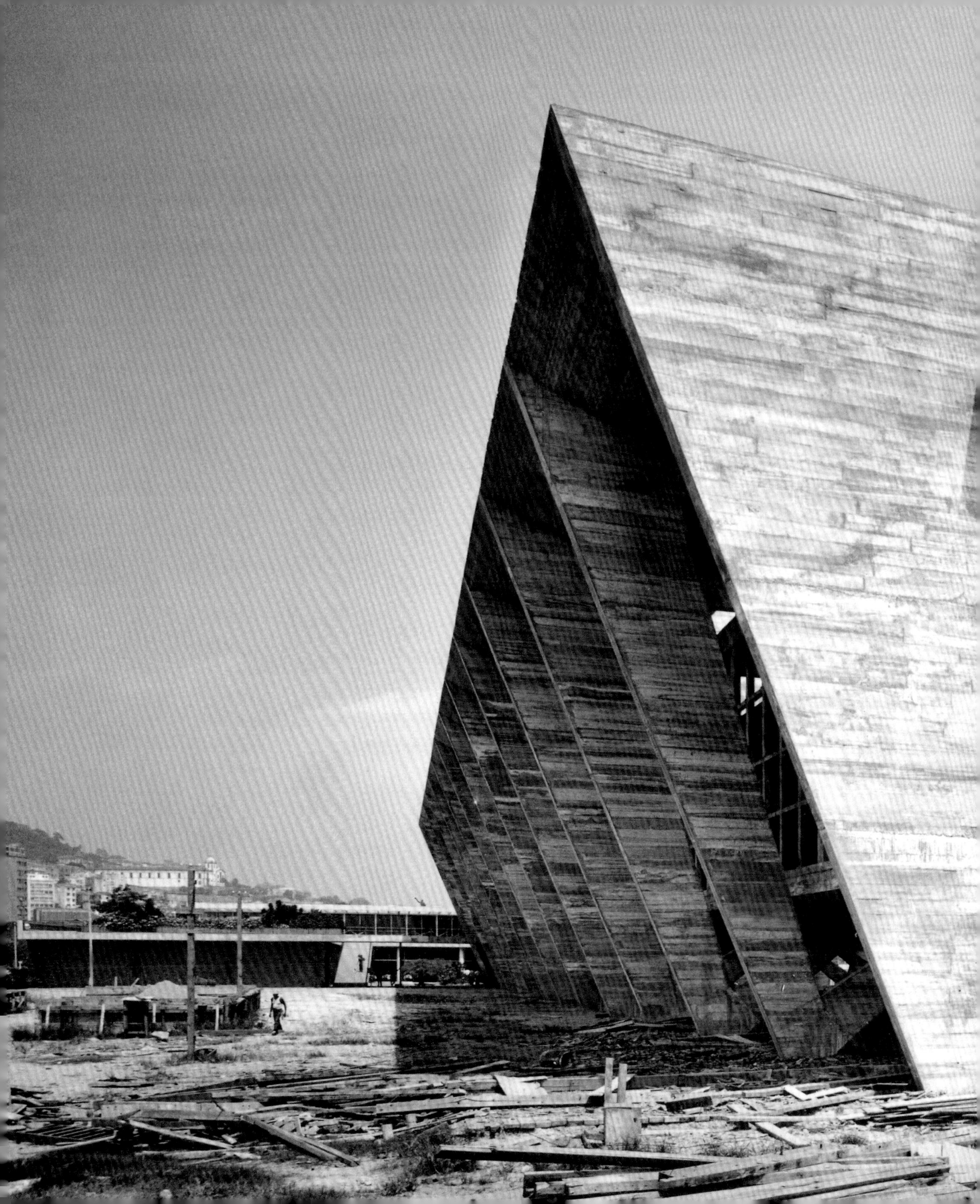

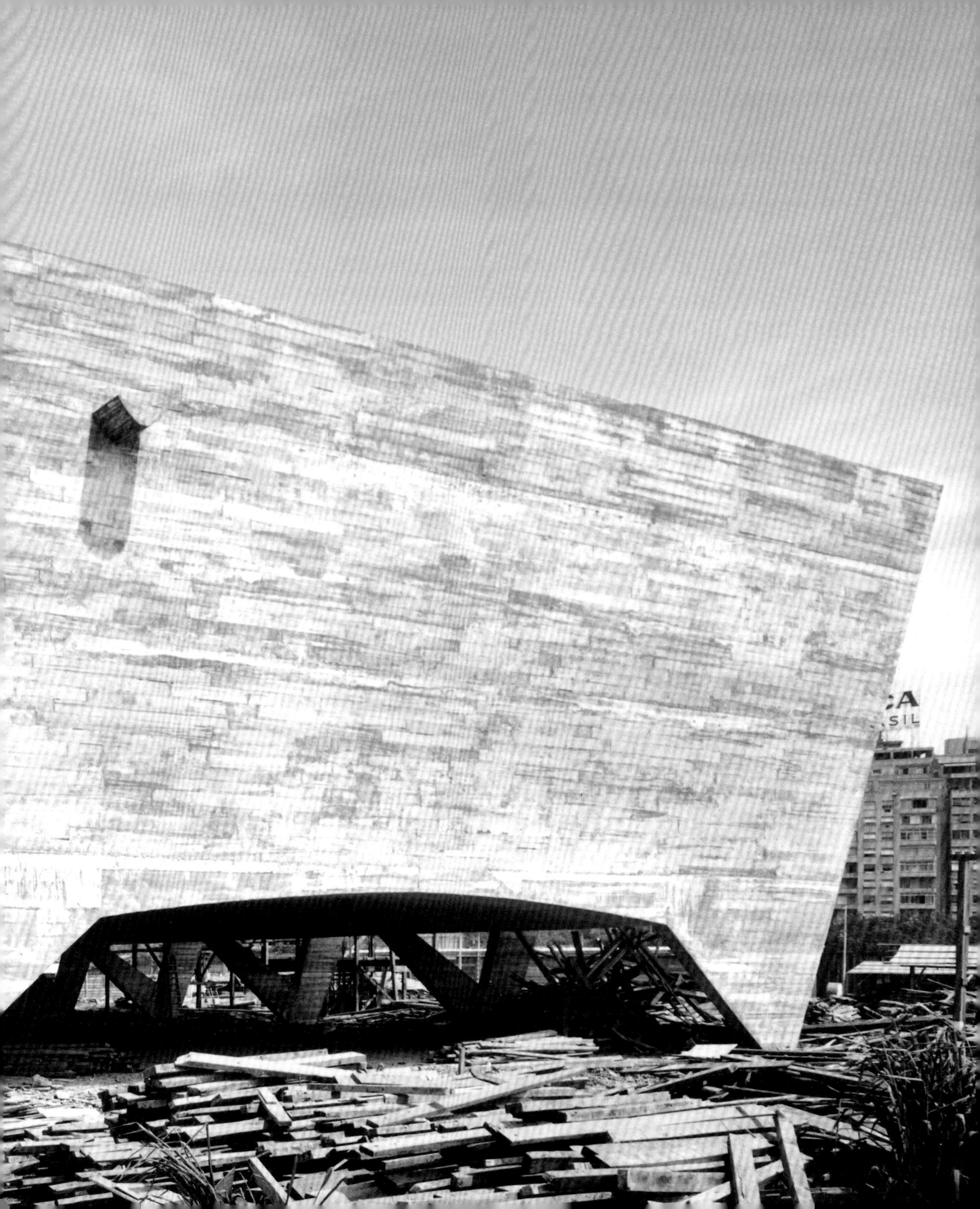

Museu de Arte Moderna Rio de Janeiro

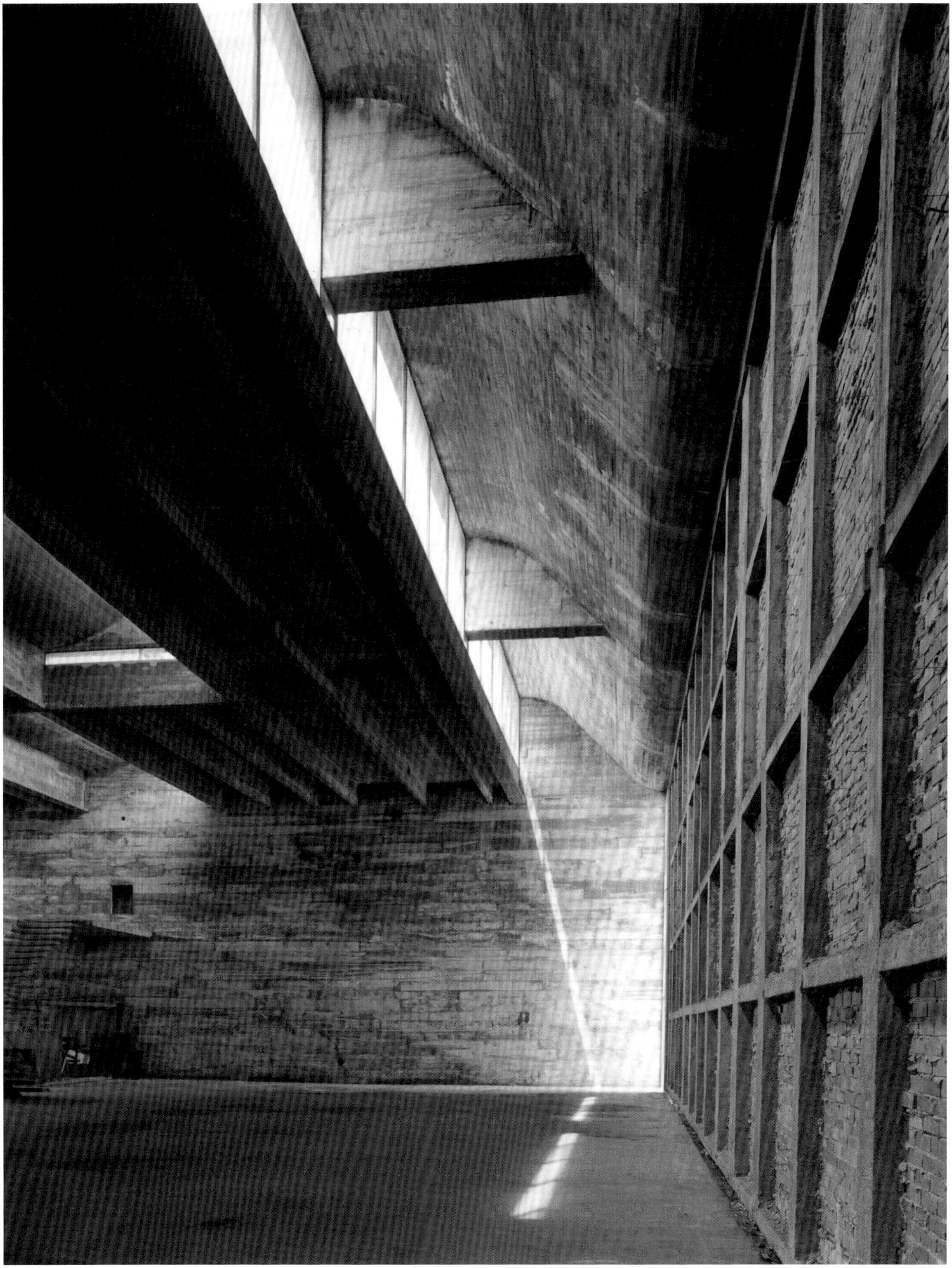

Museu de Arte Moderna Rio de Janeiro

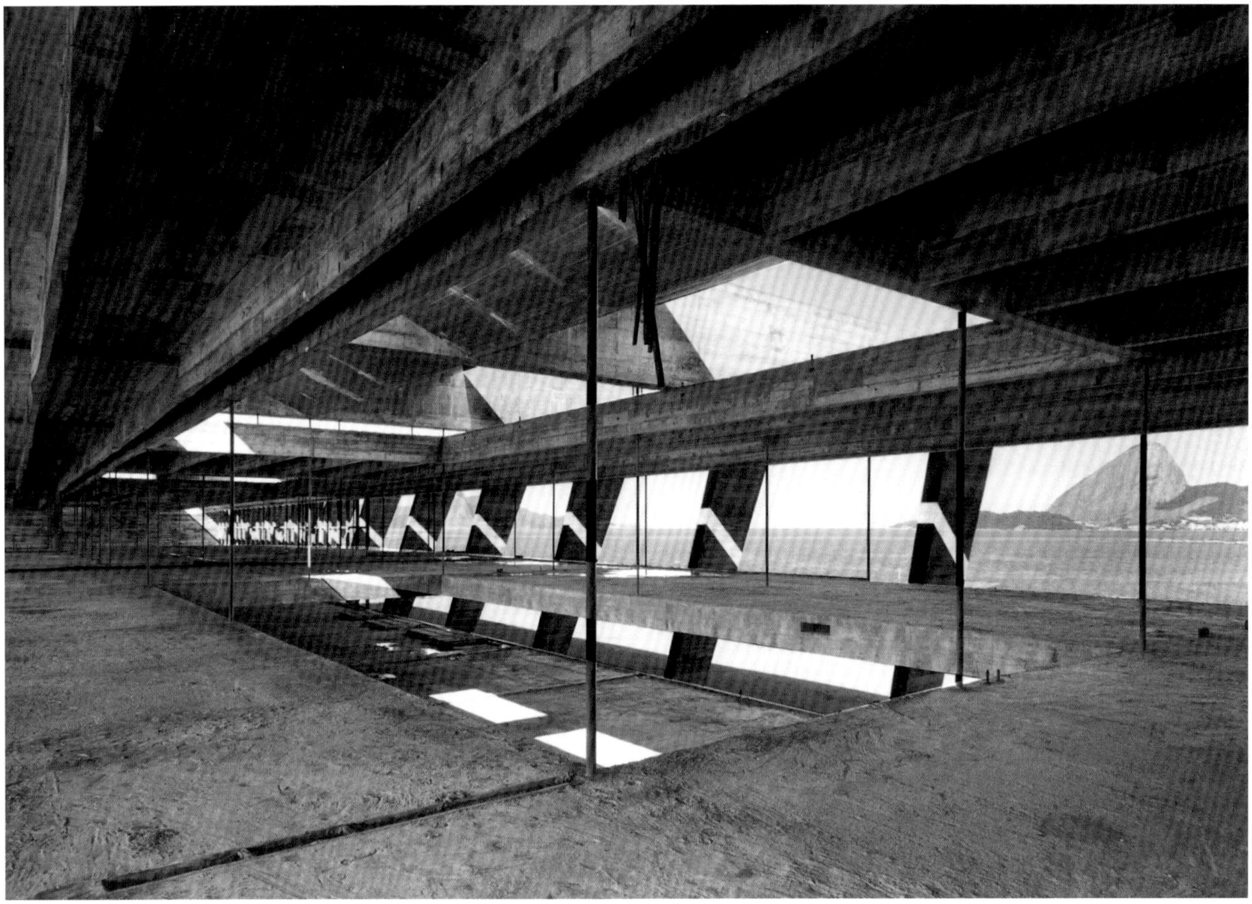

94 Museu de Arte Moderna Rio de Janeiro

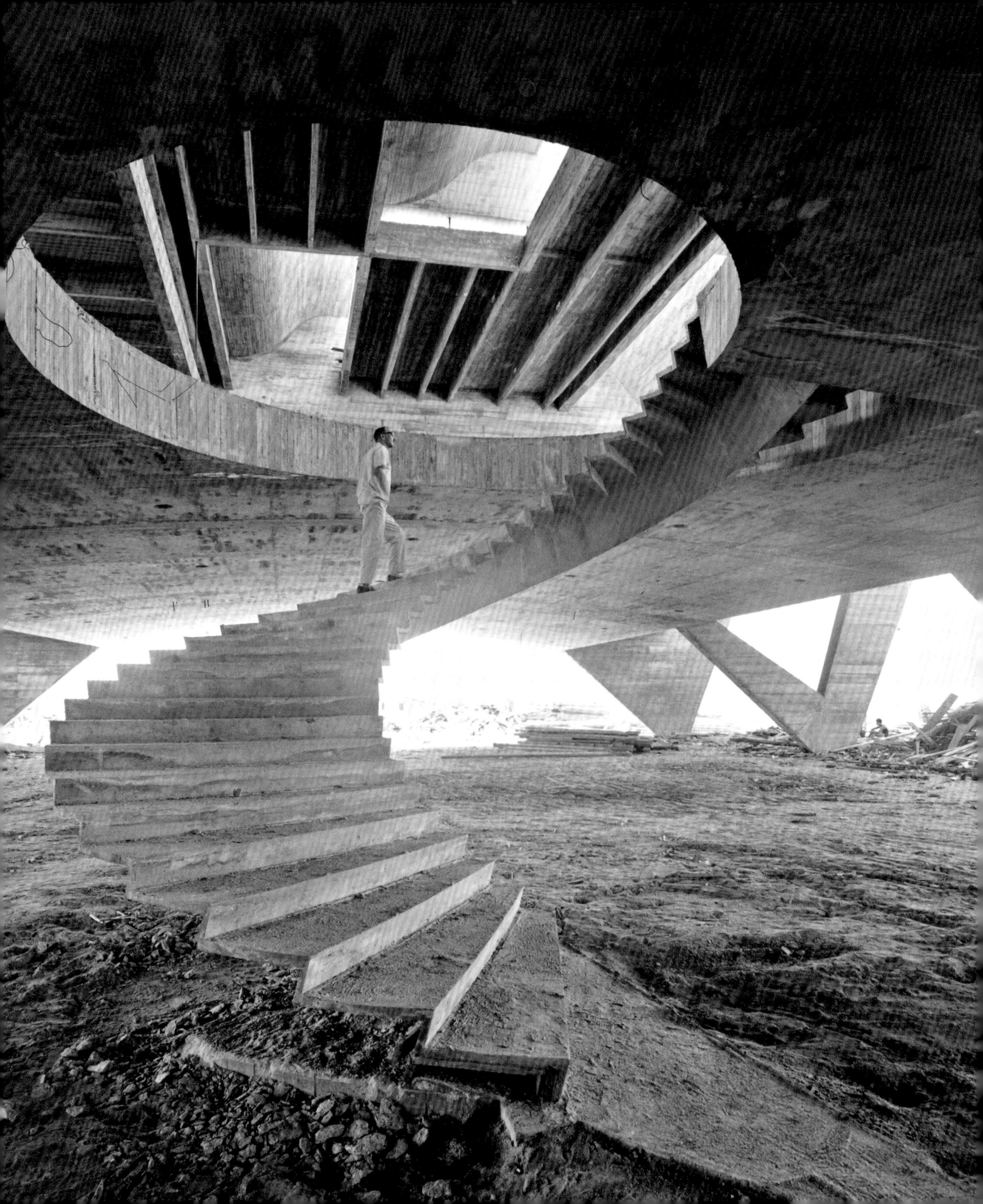

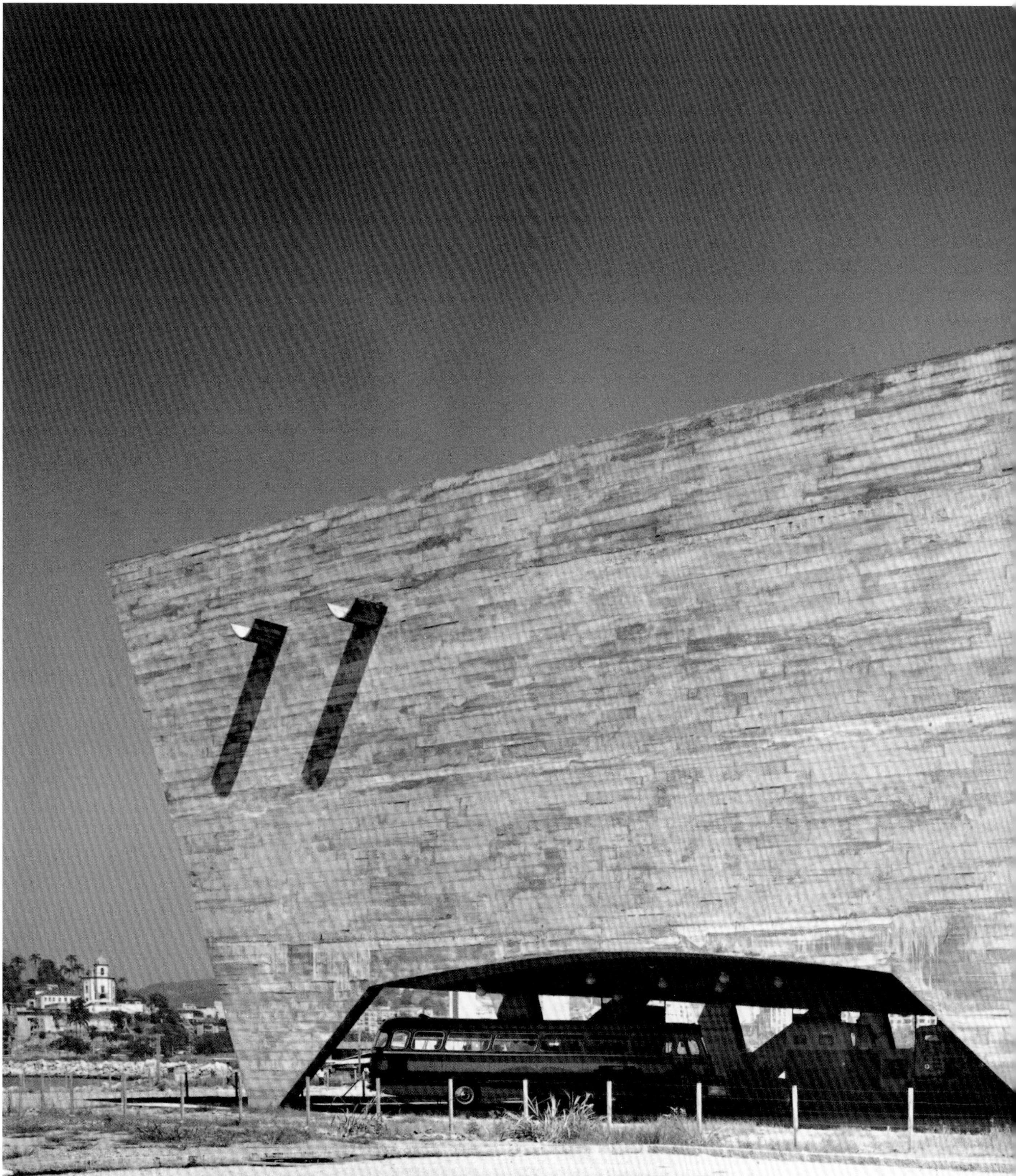

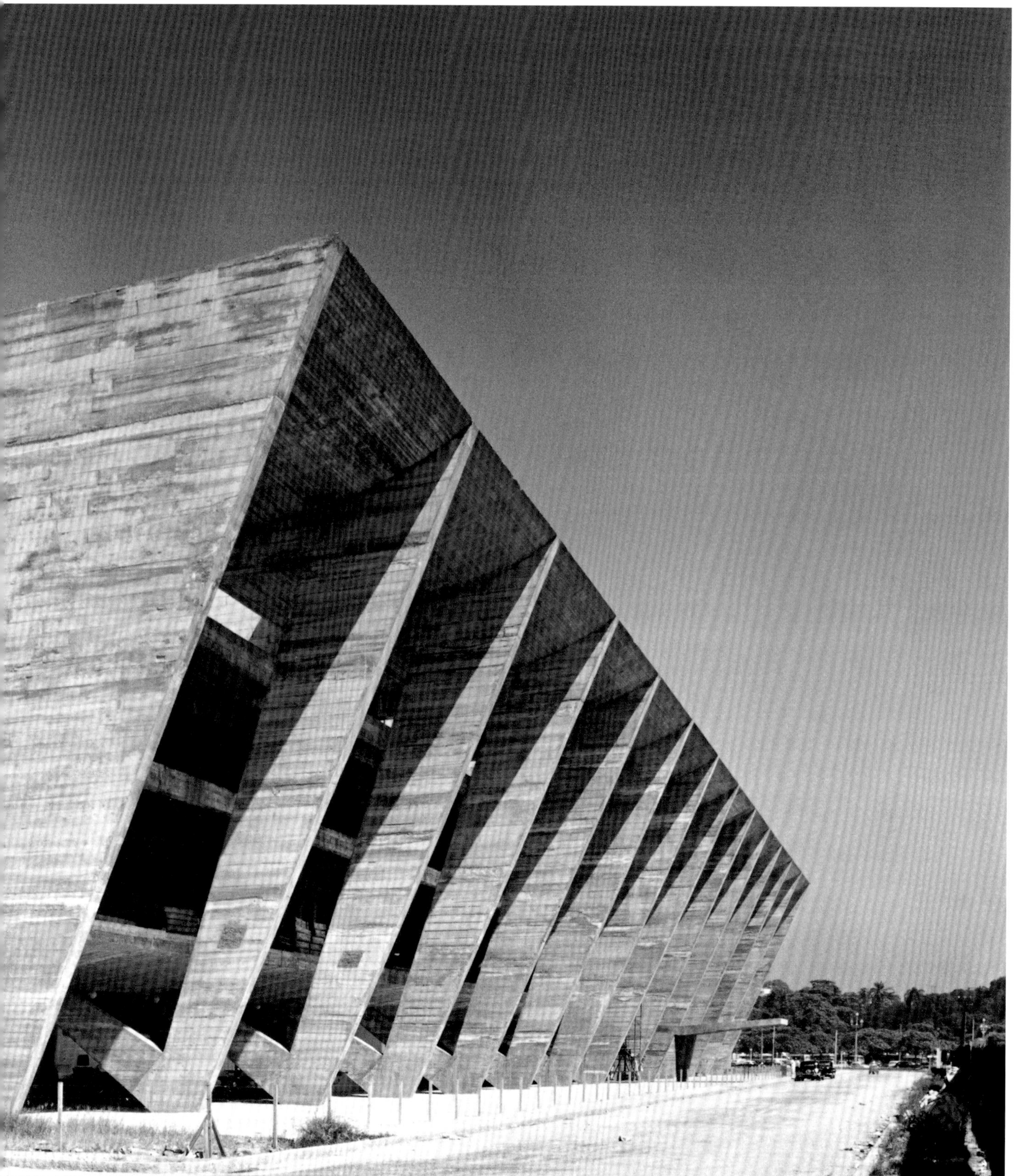

98 Museu de Arte Moderna Rio de Janeiro

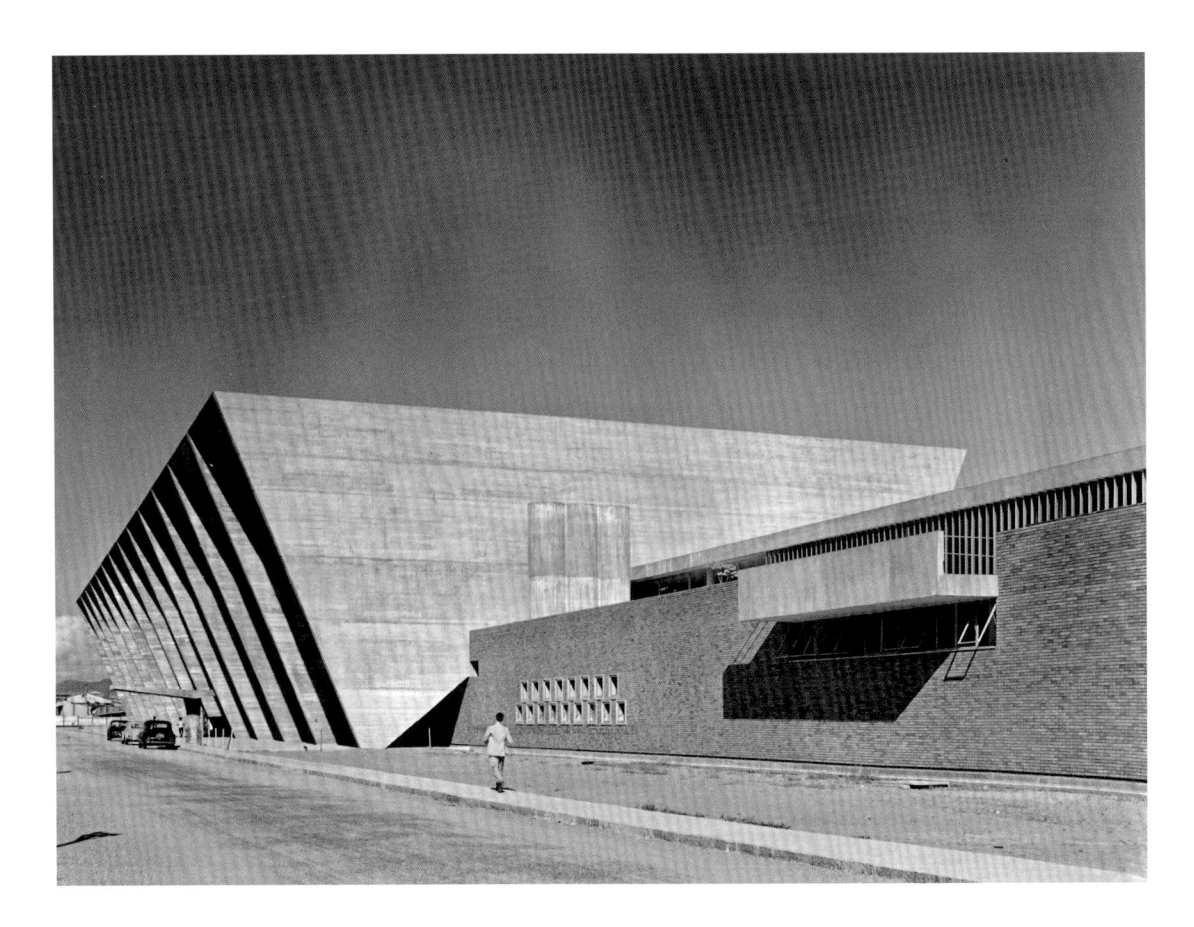

Architecture and Construction 99

School Building, Exhibition Building and Theater: the Project's Conclusion

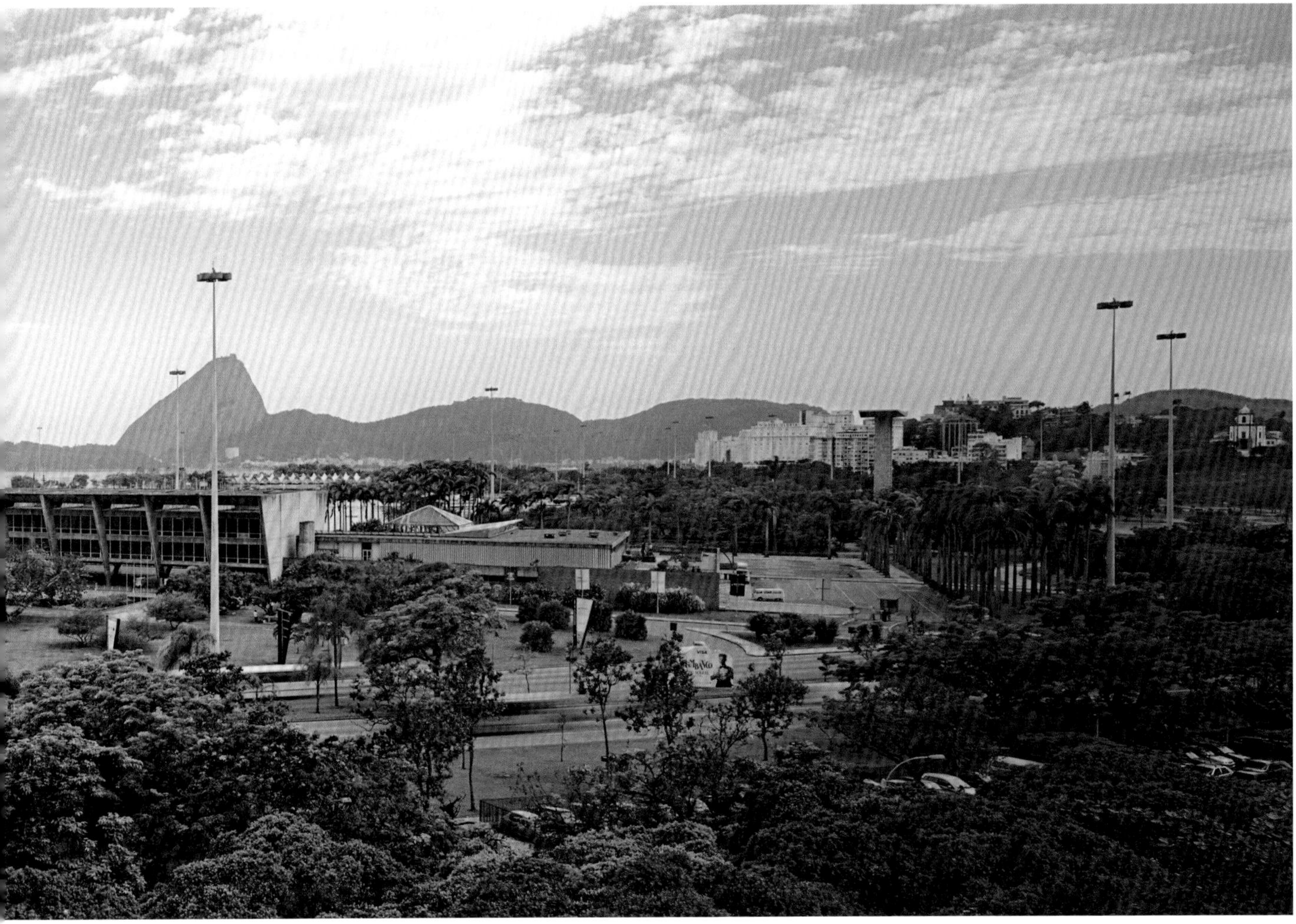

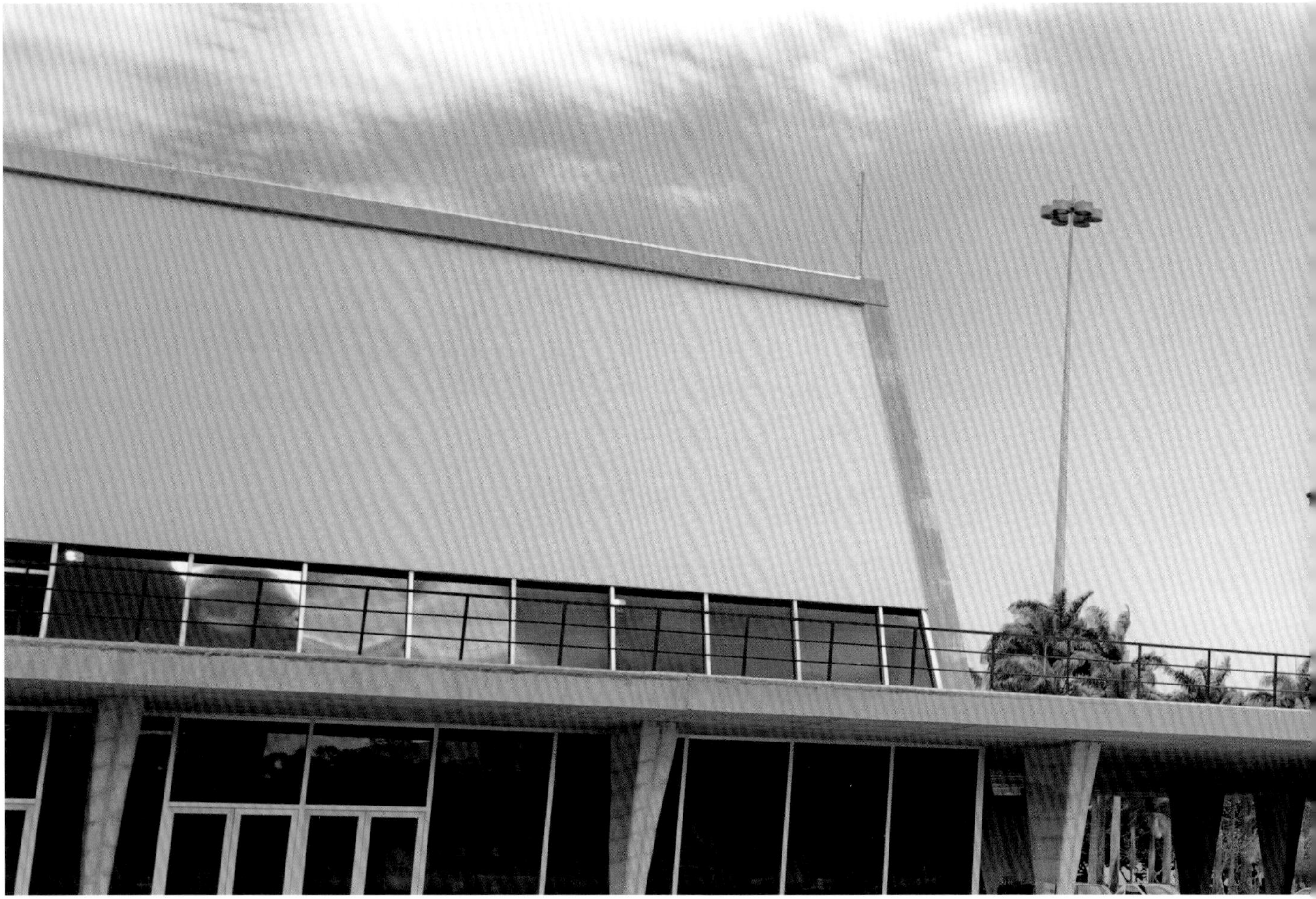

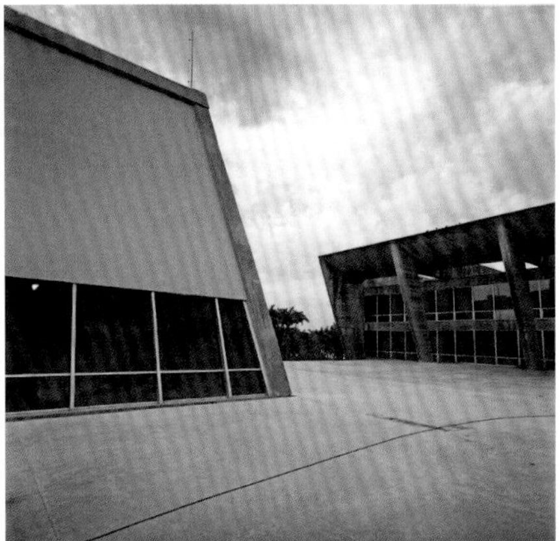

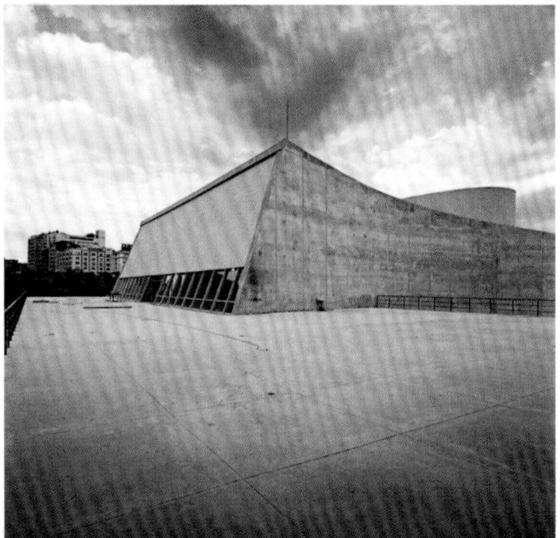

Architecture and Construction 103

Museu de Arte Moderna Rio de Janeiro

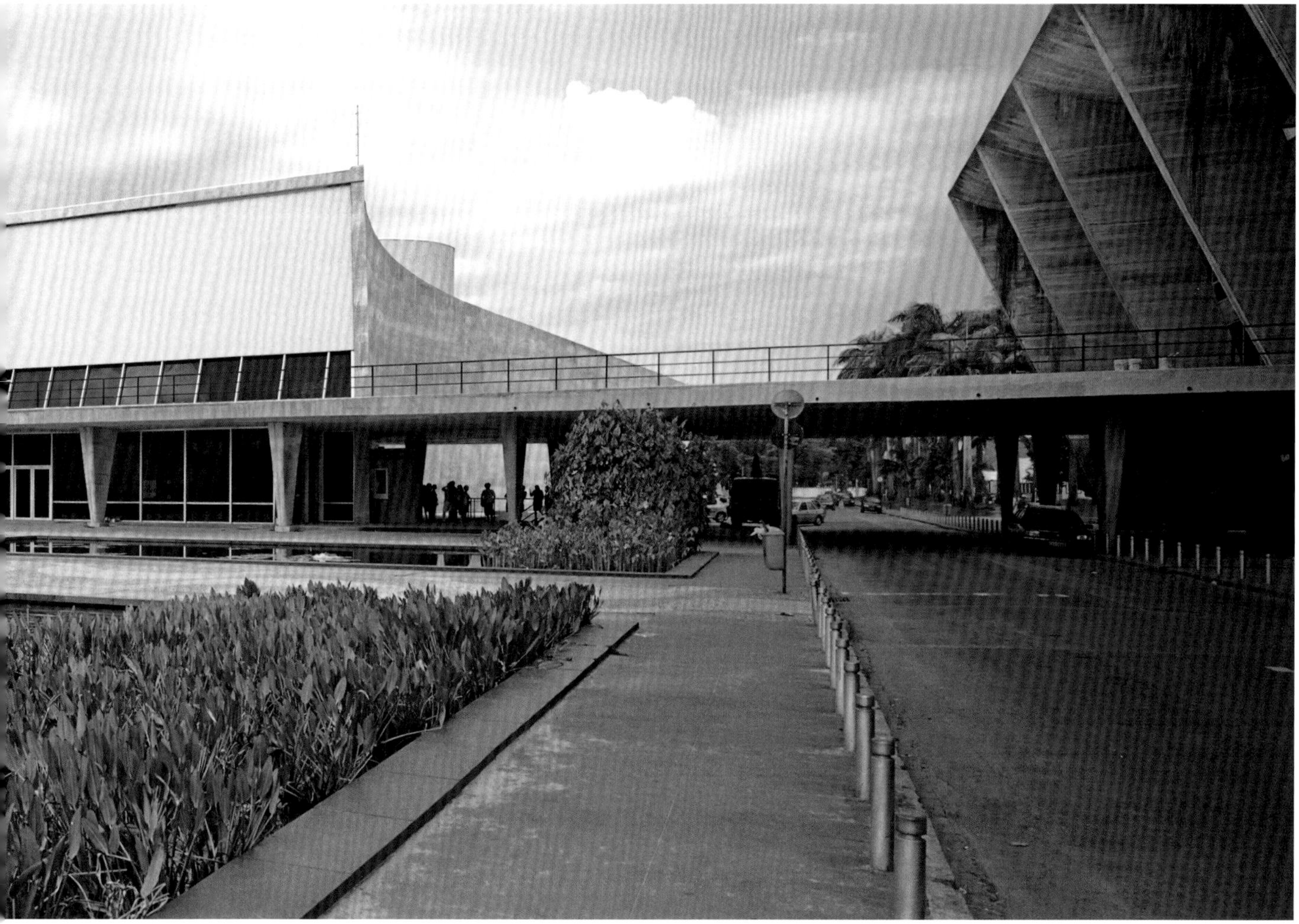

Museu de Arte Moderna Rio de Janeiro

Architecture and Construction 107

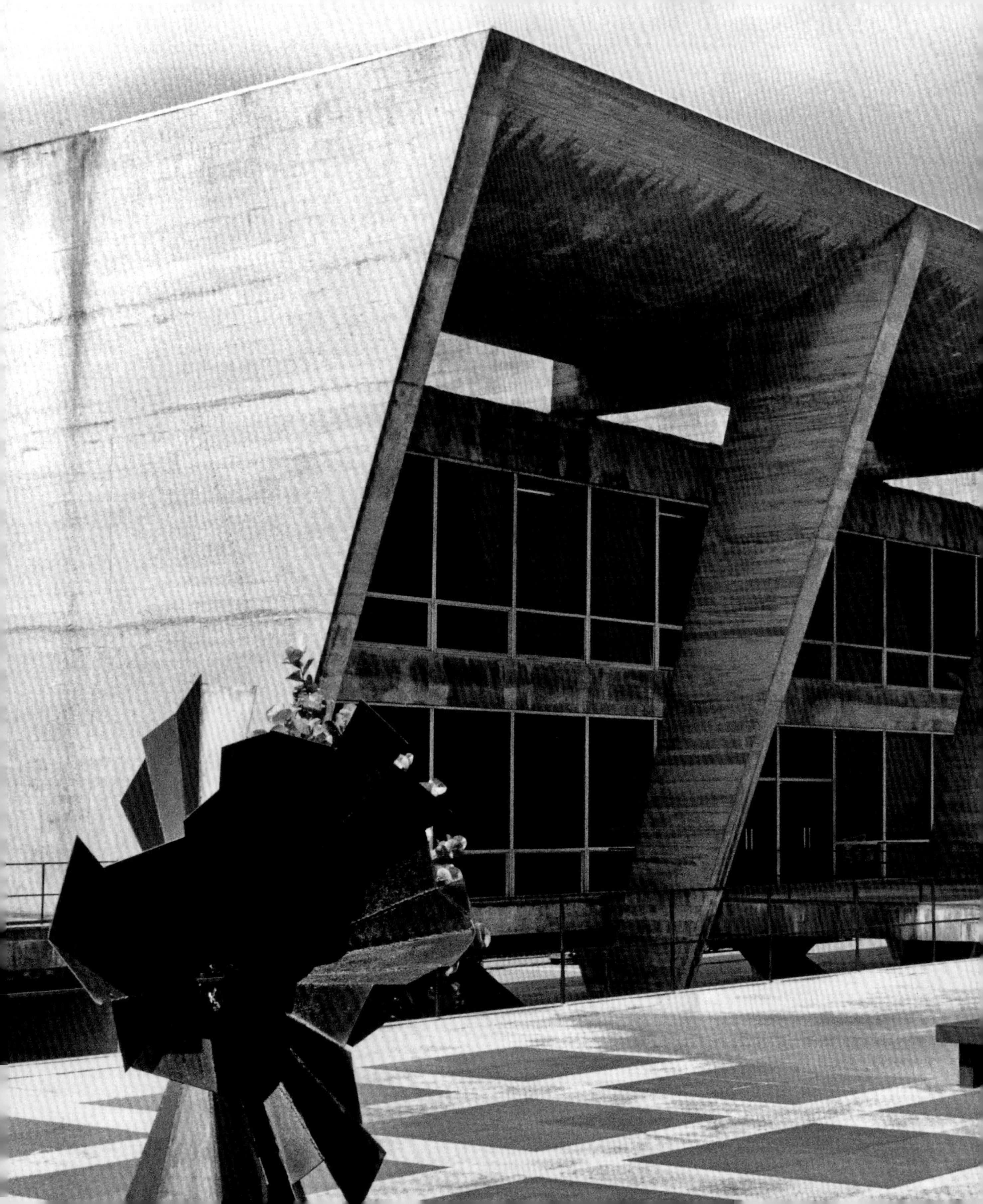

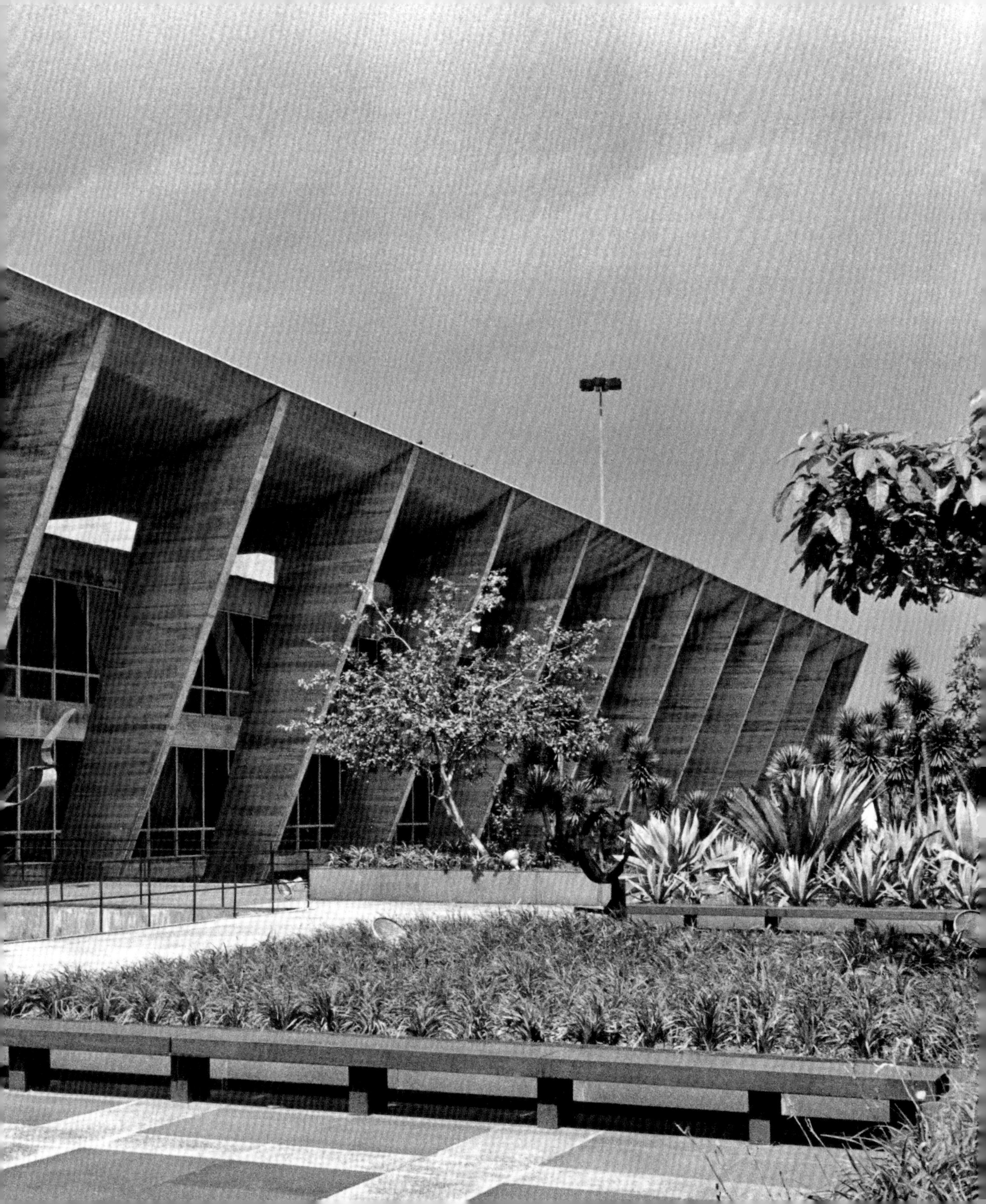

A Museum Through **Ana Luiza Nobre**

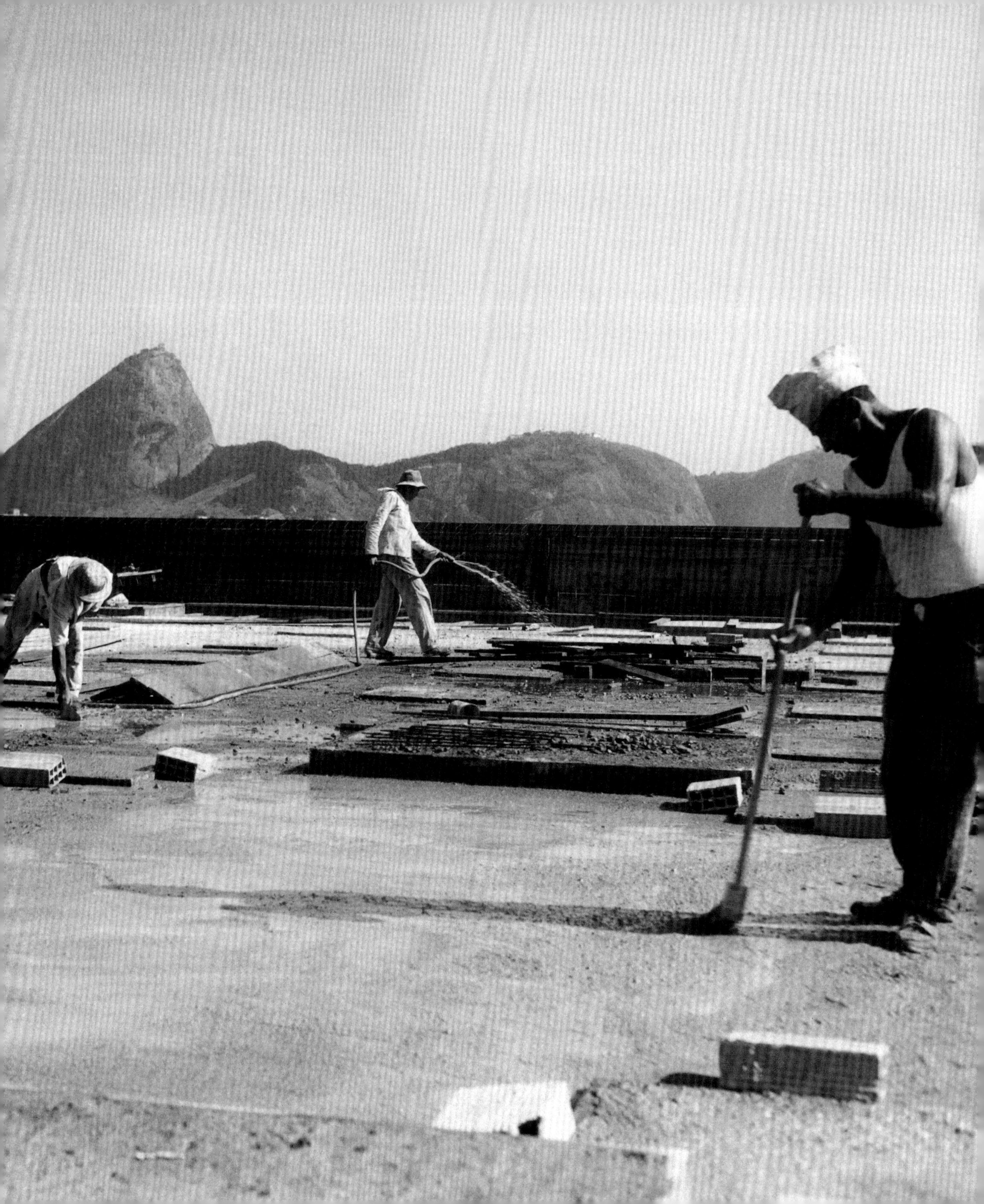

In June 1948, Affonso Eduardo Reidy (1909-64) wrote to the French architect Le Corbusier that he was working on an important urban planning project in Rio de Janeiro's city center: "Do you remember that small hill in the heart of the city where there is a convent? It is to be razed and I am making studies for the site's urbanization."[1] Reidy was referring to the Esplanade of Santo Antonio, a central area for which city hall had been examining urban planning proposals for several years and that now, finally, was about to undergo transformation. Signed by Reidy himself – then head of the city's department of urban planning – the project promised to articulate the city's North and South zones by means of an elevated expressway and foresaw the creation of a civic center that would include – among other things – a spiral-shaped museum developed at length by Le Corbusier.[2]

The enthusiastic answer soon arrived. Le Corbusier declared himself to be "salivating" with regard to the chance to design again in the "city most indicated by the gods to have a veritable architectural gem inscribed within a carefully-chosen terrain." [3] The French architect had already been in Rio twice (in 1929 and 1936) and knew that its urban center was – by then – marked by a an architectural work that surely owed a great deal to him: the building-site of the Ministry of Education and Health, recently-inaugurated on the Castelo Esplanade and designed by Lucio Costa, Oscar Niemeyer, Jorge Machado Moreira, Carlos Leão, Ernani Vasconcellos and Reidy himself (with Le Corbusier as consultant).

The period immediately following the war and the end of a long dictatorship was undoubtedly one of cultural effervescence and investment in a process of modernization of political and cultural structures. Such a process would necessarily include new art museums organized according to non-academic criteria from both museological, museographical and architectural-spatial perspectives; in other words, no longer conceived of as reliquaries meant for the storage or offering up to contemplation of works of art from the past but considered as active centers with artistic output of the present, in which traditional exhibition galleries – closed in on themselves and practically devoid of contact with the outside world – would be replaced by flexible, dynamic spaces more effectively available to the public and integrated to workshops, playhouses, film theaters, restaurants, etc.

It is within this context that the MASP (São Paulo Art Museum) and Rio de Janeiro and São Paulo's museums of Modern Art emerge in 1947 and 1948, respectively. Rio's MAM was created exactly one month prior to Reidy's letter to Le Corbusier. Dated May 3, 1948, the founding minutes defined the new museum as a nonprofit civil society "intended to put on and maintain permanent and temporary visual art exhibitions; organize a film library, a photographic art archive, specialized phonograph record collections and libraries; to promote film exhibitions of artistic and cultural interest, concerts, conferences and courses related to their aims, research on folklore and interchange with kindred foreign organizations; in short, to disseminate the knowledge of modern art in Brazil."[4]

The new museum was inaugurated in January, 1949, temporarily occupying the last floor of the Banco Boavista building – an Oscar Niemeyer project located on the equally new Presidente Vargas Avenue. A second headquarters would be established in 1952 on the pilotis of the building-site for the Ministry of Education, partially closed off by Niemeyer with wood screens to house a roughly 500 square meter large exhibition room. As part of an intensive program, Max Bill's Tripartite Unity was presented to the public of Rio along with engravings by Goya, photographs by Marcel Gautherot and projects by Lucio Costa and Sergio Bernardes, for example. Reaction was instantaneous. Over 47 thousand people visited the museum from January to December of that year. Its success contributed to the consolidation of an idea that had been growing throughout 1952 – the creation of a definitive site for the MAM. Finally, in November, the city donated a 40 thousand square meter area to the museum. The terrain itself, however, was yet to materialize for, at that point, it was only a section of Guanabara Bay awaiting landfill from the razing of Santo Antônio Hill.[5]

It was, therefore, upon water that the project's earliest sketches emerged, entrusted, as it had been, to Reidy and, from the outset, inscribed as part of his propositions for Rio. According to the architect, the new museum was conceived as a result of its privileged location: "[…] within the very heart of the city, in the midst of a vast area that is soon to be a beautiful public park overlooking the sea and facing the entrance to the bar and encircled by the world's most beautiful landscape." The purpose of avoiding any disturbance to this landscape defines the architectural directive: "predominantly horizontal lines counterposed to the busy outline of the mountain range and the employment of a thoroughly pierced, transparent structure that would allow its garden to continue through the building itself all the way to the sea."[6] Clearly influenced by Le Corbusier, this directive is summed up in a series of sketches in which Reidy schematically presents the arrangement of the exhibition gallery upon an elevated platform intended to create an unobstructed view of the ground level.

Earlier, in 1952, Reidy had applied a similar solution to the Brazil-Paraguay Experimental School, in Asunción. In that project – which occupies terrain overlooking a river – the architect also freed up the ground level as much as possible by employing an apparent concrete structure to modulate the school block's northern façade and compose a system with a sun baffle. In this sense, it might be said that the Paraguayan school somehow foreshadows the Rio de Janeiro museum. And yet, in the Museu de Arte Moderna do Rio de Janeiro's case, what actually resolves the project is the great cohesiveness between the complex of buildings, the natural landscape and the city. Allowing this particular project to be crossed through by the city is a decision that will have inevitable consequences for the architecture (that will become inseparable from the urban flow) and for the city (that will once again extend its boundaries beyond and through the building to the sea).

It may be said that a cultural, architectural and civic fact is consummated there, one that does not affirm itself by contrast with the radiant nature of Rio but, instead, by playing "a game for two,"[7] in Le Corbusier's own words. Once more, the museum emphatically intervenes upon nature, thus closing a circle of sorts that began with Le Corbusier or, earlier still, with Pereira Passos.[8] Erected upon a site that is isolated from the urban grid, its fundamental strategy consists in seeking out a continuity that occurs not through any direct connection with traditional urban spaces – which would be untenable, given the terrain's insular nature – but by making use of public and eminently urban surroundings that the great shadow underneath the exhibition gallery recovers and reinvents, by the sea. Thus, the project allows itself to be read almost as a commentary on the unusual nature of this city, permanently transformed and re-transformed by man's action upon a previously formless and unmapped territory. This is because it synthesizes the permanent tension between the construction and destruction of cities, the triumphant invention of an urbanity that projects itself, free of thresholds, from the museum and far beyond it, redefining (and re-territorializing) everything that exists or is about to emerge around it: the high-speed lanes of Flamengo Park and the overpasses that leap over them, Burle Marx's landscaping, the little church of Glória, Sugar Loaf, Guanabara Bay and the Rio-Niterói bridge.

In this process, architecture might run the risk of depleting itself of itself. But no, of course not. The architectural artifact is there, limpid and irreducible, radiating a power that only architecture possesses and technique allows.

Structure and Plasticity

With its portico structure made up of 14 porticos of reinforced concrete that repeat themselves every ten meters, the exhibition block's 130 meter expanse is clearly defined as the dominant body of the architectural composition. Its dialogue with Mies van der Rohe's structural logic is clearly revealed here. With its 39 meter free span, 16,93 meter height and 2,70 meter high main beam, the profile of the portico designed by the architect retains the monumental quality associated with traditional museums even as it renders viable the structural challenge calculated by engineer Arthur Jermann: rather than being supported upon pillars, the intermediate and rooftop flagstones hang from steel cables within the main beam of the main panel so as to keep the 26 by 130 meter exhibition hall free of columns, thus allowing great flexibility in the mounting of exhibitions.

In order to guarantee the structure's sturdiness, the elements that make up the panels are longitudinally interconnected by overhangs of an approximate 8 meter width that perform the function of shuttering even as they protect the façade from direct sunlight. Additionally, 14 balance beams executed in prestressed concrete (and calculated by Bruno Contarini) interconnect the panels transversally underground.

Entirely executed in apparent concrete to which a sense of dynamism is imparted by a combination of horizontal and oblique lines, the structure is exploited in its plasticity and its serial elements define the museum's very image. The numbers associated with its execution are impressive. According to a report by engineer and construction foreman Fuad Kanan Matta, the framework for the main beam alone consumed 45 tons of iron, sufficient to execute the structure of a 12-story building. [9] The painstaking construction work also required surfaced lumber molds executed with a tongue and groove system so as to leave only the slightest joint line apparent. This was because, in his synchronic elaboration of the building's most intimate scale with the city's largest one, Reidy was as careful about defining the portico's monumental proportions as he was in controlling all of the detail and final touches with a constructive rigor that reached the extreme of demanding, for instance, alignment of the door and window frames with the joints between the bricks, the marble of the flooring and the pillar, of the electric switch and the tile.

Functional Sectorization

The program's organization into plastically differentiated and discontinuous albeit communicating volumes – exhibitions, school and theater – ensures the immediate apprehension of each one of these functions by the pedestrian who approaches the museum from the bridge (also designed by Reidy) that looks out onto it or by the sweeping gaze from a moving car. On the other hand, this distinction also allowed for each one of the blocks to be independently executed. And it was surely no accident that construction began with the School Block and not the Exhibition Block, as might have been expected. It was a way of signaling the importance assigned to the educational function of an institution whose primary reference was New York's MoMA/Museum of Modern Art and would soon establish ties with the HfG/Hochschule für Gestaltung – the design school created in Ulm, Germany, as a sort of postwar echo of the Bauhaus.

Between 1958 (when the museum's new site was inaugurated) and 1967 (when the Exhibition Block was finally concluded), all exhibitions were held in the School Block. They included epochal shows such as the First Neoconcrete Exhibition that defined the bifurcation of concrete art in Brazil (in 1959) and the Opinião 65 show at which Hélio Oiticica burst forth into the museum's spaces with his parangolés (in 1965).

By the time the Exhibition Block was concluded, Reidy had been dead for several years. The ambiance generated by the lighting system originally conceived by the architect, combining natural light (through windows and sheds) and artificial light (both incandescent and fluorescent) was modified over time, as were several of the museum's spaces. Nor did Reidy live long enough to see the MAM fire in 1978 (which destroyed a large part of its collection although it did not compromise its structure). Neither did he witness the Theater's controversial conclusion in 2006.

In spite of all this, the museum retains its most precious asset: the civic character given to it by Reidy. Its architecture continues to move us in its correspondence between nature and the city; the former continually tamed by technique, the latter understood in its essentially political – and for this very reason vital – dimension of human existence.

Ana Luiza Nobre
May 2010

1 Letter from Affonso Eduardo Reidy to Le Corbusier, June 7, 1948, in Bonduki, N. *Affonso Eduardo Reidy*. São Paulo/Lisbon: Instituto Lina Bo e Pietro Maria Bardi/Editorial Blau, 1999, p. 21. (Free translation by the author).
2 Le Corbusier's concept for a spiral-shaped museum dates back to the early 1920s (with the Mundaneum and the World Museum); he continued to elaborate it during the 1930s (in the Museum of Contemporary Art in Paris and the "museum of unlimited growth"). See Boesinger, W. and Girsberger, H. *Le Corbusier 1910-65*. Barcelona: Gustavo Gili, 1971.
3 Undated letter from Le Corbusier to Affonso Eduardo Reidy. Carmen Portinho collection. (Free translation by the author)
4 Apud Nobre, Ana Luiza. *Carmen Portinho: o Moderno em Construção*. Rio de Janeiro: Relume Dumará, 1999, p. 71.
5 Then known as the so-called Aterro de Santa Luzia [Santa Luzia Landfill], the second landfill near the church of that name, which had already been moved away from the sea by the razing of Castelo Hill in the 1920s. See Abreu, Maurício de. *Evolução urbana do Rio de Janeiro*. Rio de Janeiro: Iplanrio/Zahar, 1987.
6 Reidy, Affonso Eduardo. Memorial Descritivo do Museu de Arte Moderna do Rio de Janeiro. Apud Bonduki, Nabil. Op. Cit. p. 164.
7 Le Corbusier. *Precisões sobre um estado presente da arquitetura e do urbanismo*. São Paulo: Cosac Naify, 2004. p. 229.
8 I am referring to the urban reforms that took place between 1902 and 1906 by Mayor Francisco Pereira Passos, when the city of Rio de Janeiro underwent profound morphological and territorial modifications in an effort to divest itself of its colonial features. See Benchimol, Jaime Larry. *Pereira Passos: um Haussmann tropical. A renovação urbana na cidade do Rio de Janeiro no início do século XX*. Rio de Janeiro: Secretaria Municipal de Cultura, Turismo e Esportes, 1992.
9 Matta, Fuad Kanan. "As obras do Museu. Relatório do Engenheiro" in Boletim do MAM, number 17, January, 1959.

Ana Luiza Nobre is an architect, academic and author. She teaches in the specialization course on the History of Art and Architecture in Brazil and in the graduate course in Architecture, both at PUC-Rio.

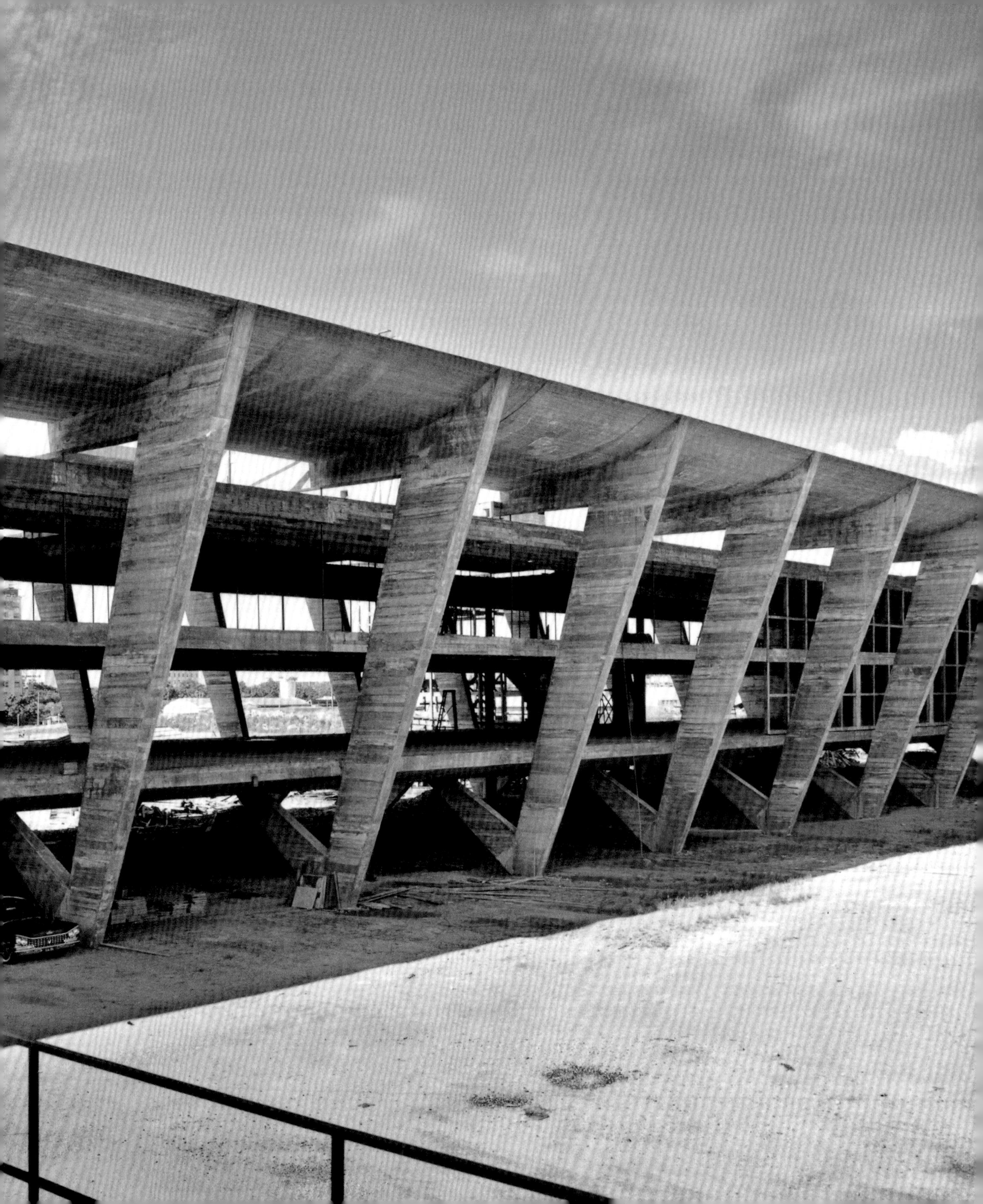

Statement   **Paulo Mendes da Rocha**

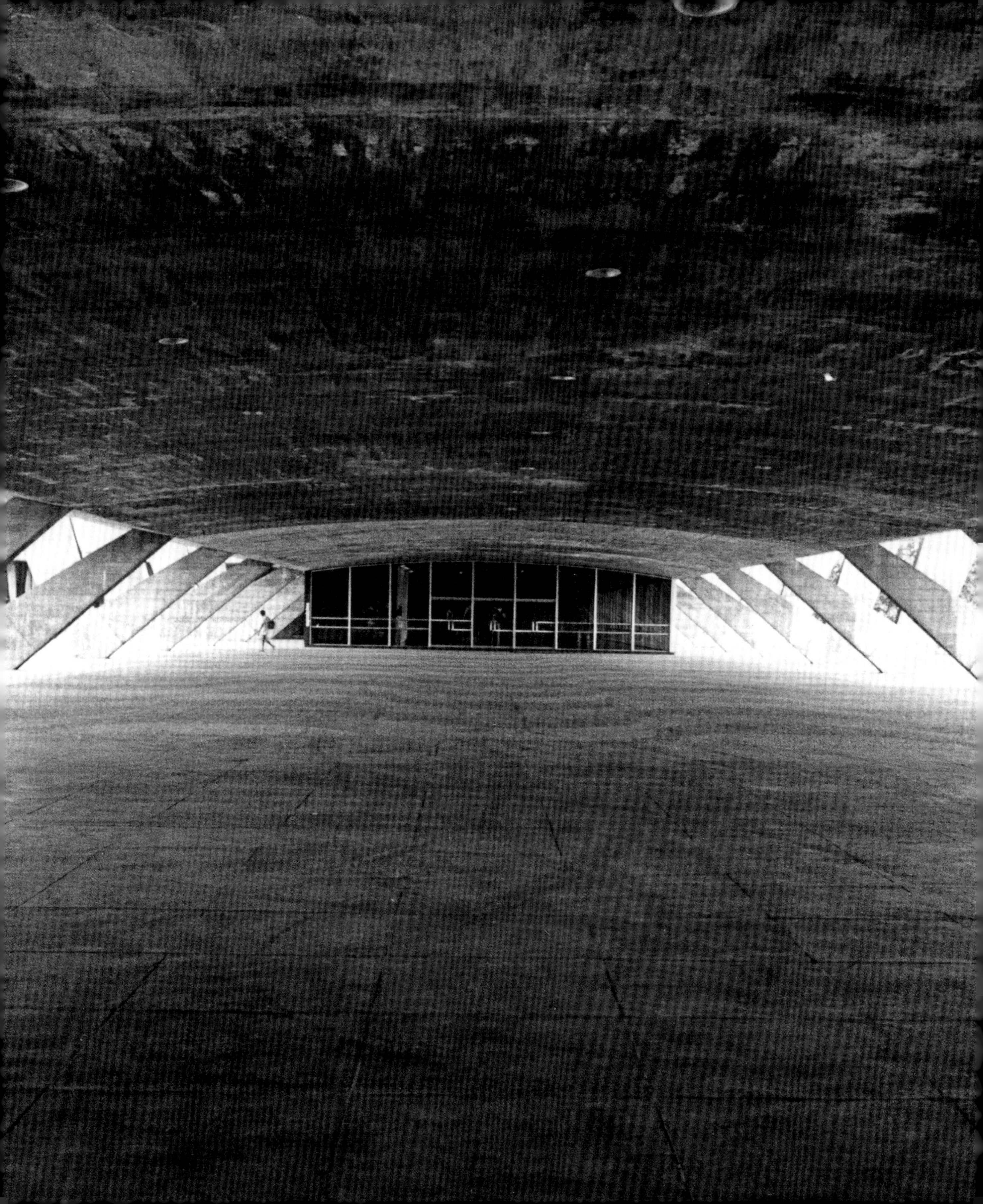

In order to speak of Affonso Eduardo Reidy, I must take a good look at the city of Rio de Janeiro – a spectacle, a clear discourse on the transformation of nature. In this new, constructed place the figure of the carioca also emerged as one who sings "and a window looking out on the sea (…) how lovely!": a character who knows that nature is worth nothing without the window. This architectural awareness of where we are – vague and diffuse though it may be, is yet charged with lyrical and poetic meaning and with a strength that one sees also in the *favelas* – is (and was) in my education, a seductive and particular – let us say Brazilian – mark: a disconcerting and active force at once popular and erudite.

There is an ongoing debate about whether or not a Brazilian architecture exists – which it should, at any rate, as a way to challenge construction in this new world called America. Modernity emerges with Galileo and Columbus and, we might also add, with Palladio, a physicist, navigator and architect who said that "the city would no longer be that of classical antiquity, made of monuments, for humanity would now see the emergence of the monumentality of the city." He was speaking of a Venice that would be built in the heart of Europe as a result of the newborn wealth of trade and navigation, albeit within the fragile territory of an inappropriate lagoon in the confined spaces of the Adriatic and devoid of any natural charm.

Nature as phenomenon – geographical location, the mechanics of fluids, the mechanics of soils – rather than as mere landscape. For the extraordinary beauty of Guanabara Bay is also unsettling! This Rio de Janeiro that gains from the sea, dredging operations and junctions, landfills and drainage systems. Works of engineering. How ought one to inhabit such a beautiful place? How to approach this landscape, this monumental topography, all of this gigantic granite? The first step was to name it all in a domestic, conciliatory fashion – the comfortable Gávea district, hills and rocks named after two brothers, a pan, a little hunchback, a sugar loaf… In the meantime, the city provided a Central Avenue, a Rio Branco Avenue, with a port at one extreme and an airport at another to support implantation of the Senate (Monroe), the Museu de Belas Artes, the Biblioteca Nacional, the Theatro Municipal, the Ministry of Education and Culture, the Banco do Brasil and Candelária Cathedral – a perpendicular axis to the soft curve of the beaches along which the houses stand. Remarkable constructions that reconfigure the entire territory. The draining of the Mangue Canal, the construction of the Getúlio Vargas Avenue, the razing of Castelo Hill and the urbanization of the wide space of the Castelo Esplanade, with the pleasant use of the shadow-drenched arcades…

In addition to its small canal and bridge, construction of the airport on the sea further refines the Island of Villegaignon and the Naval School. An extraordinary caprice between nature and construction. The 1940s expansion of Copacabana's sands was a remarkable endeavor I had the pleasure of observing.

From the 1930s to the 1960s, Affonso Eduardo Reidy dedicated himself to countless urban planning projects for this extraordinary city. As for the "modern movement" in architecture, it owes its world development to the October Revolution. The social dimension of architecture, of urban planning, the idea of a city for all is the clear horizon of the matter. The Pedregulho is one of the most intelligent examples of a residential complex – from its implantation and architecture as well as in terms of the city and its geography – and the Brazil-Paraguay Covenant School, on the banks of the river in the city of Asunción, among the most beautiful works of that country's architecture. In the Flamengo Landfill, Reidy's partnership with Burle Marx is a new and extraordinary setting in that city – it may now be said – so beautiful by nature. As a building, the MAM is irreplaceable in the education of Brazilian architects and its stimulating creative and constructivist power has marked the architecture from São Paulo and influenced all subsequent generations.

What is known as "our architecture" is inconceivable without the vivid presence of this architect from Rio de Janeiro. In my own education, the MAM represents a constructed structure that is exemplary in the way it is suspended from the ground, reconfiguring a large area in which interior and exterior situations are articulated to produce spaces of uncommon beauty and controlled scale between a monumental landscape and gorgeous and unexpected inner places – always and still upon city ground – and, once again, the gardens of Burle Marx.

Its counterpoint with an annex – a recurring figure in the architecture of many ages – is most elegant and fortuitous and incredibly efficient in the arrangement of the cafeteria and restaurant spaces: it is not easy to describe how that powerfully theatrical sense of movement is achieved. The transparent structure is suspended by the reinforced and prestressed concrete porticos, and fully resolved in the two lateral rafters. It provides a beautiful counterpoint to the empty transversal spaces.

The museum – the architecture – begins in the far distance at the pedestrian passageway over the Beira-Mar Avenue, which creates a soft undulation upon which the museum may be sighted from the construction's highest point with the Sugar Loaf mountain in the background. The descending portion of the bridge leads visitors to the shade of the suspended construction, hiding the landscape which emerges anew as one approaches the museum's inner gardens on the other side. I have accompanied dear friends – among them distinguished visitors such as Luigi Snozzi – who were deeply moved by it and suggested a comprehensive publication about its construction.

In addition to its unique contribution to twentieth century architecture, all of Reidy's work – the houses – is extremely beautiful and powerful. Its ethical dimension currently imbues it with renewed value at a time in which there appears to be a certain degenerate tendency to advertising and speculation that adds nothing to the idea of architecture as a unique form of knowledge. Us and the planet. Architecture and Nature. I did not have the privilege of knowing Reidy personally. We miss him – all of us – for he left us too soon and we shall never be able to measure the magnitude of his loss.

Paulo Mendes da Rocha
May 2010

Paulo Mendes da Rocha is an architect, urbanist and academic. His work and trajectory are of utmost importance to Brazilian and world architecture. The awards bestowed upon him by numerous countries throughout his career include the prestigious Mies van der Rohe Prize for Latin America (2001) and the Pritzker Prize (in 2006).

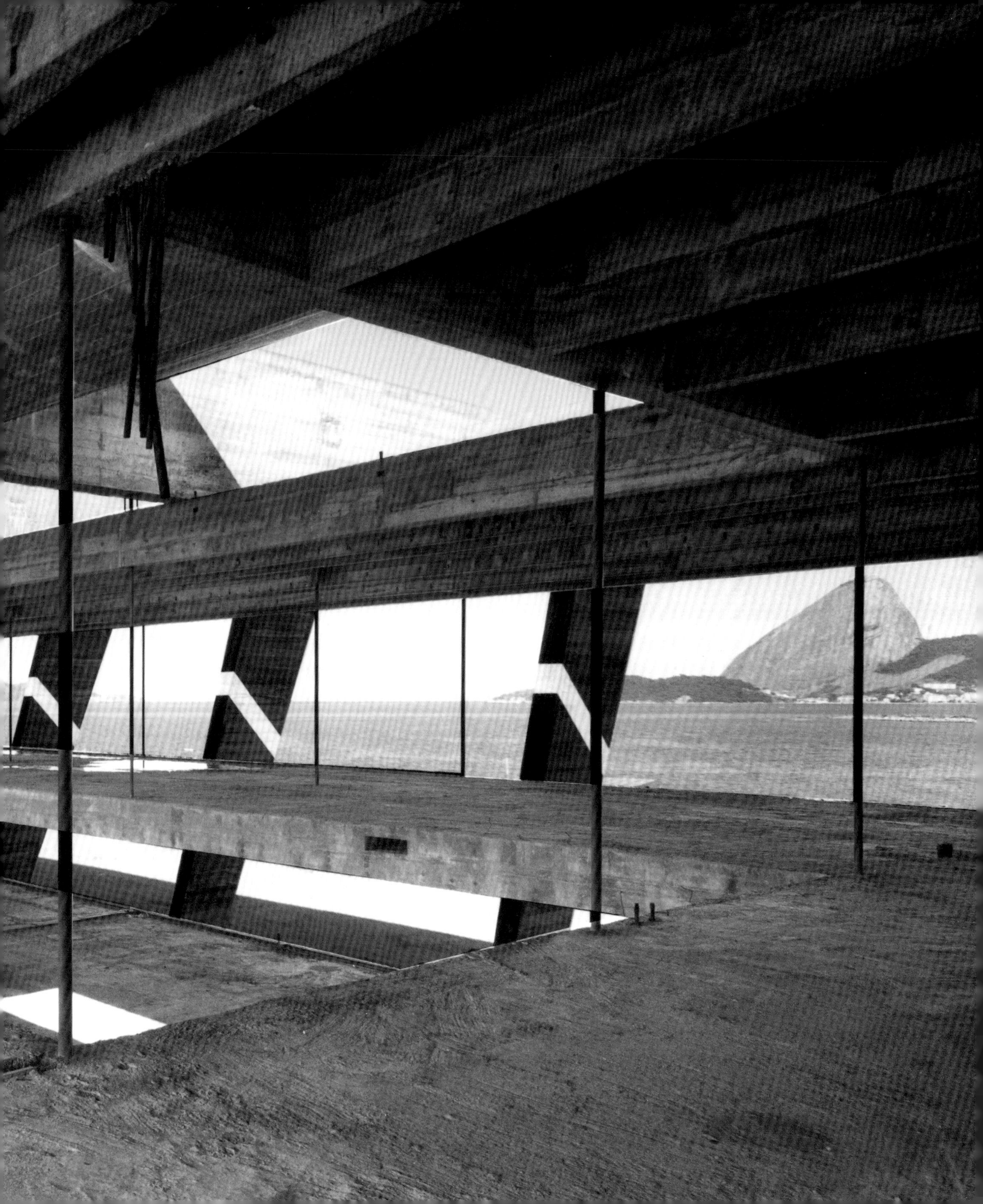

Photographic Essay **Vicente de Mello**

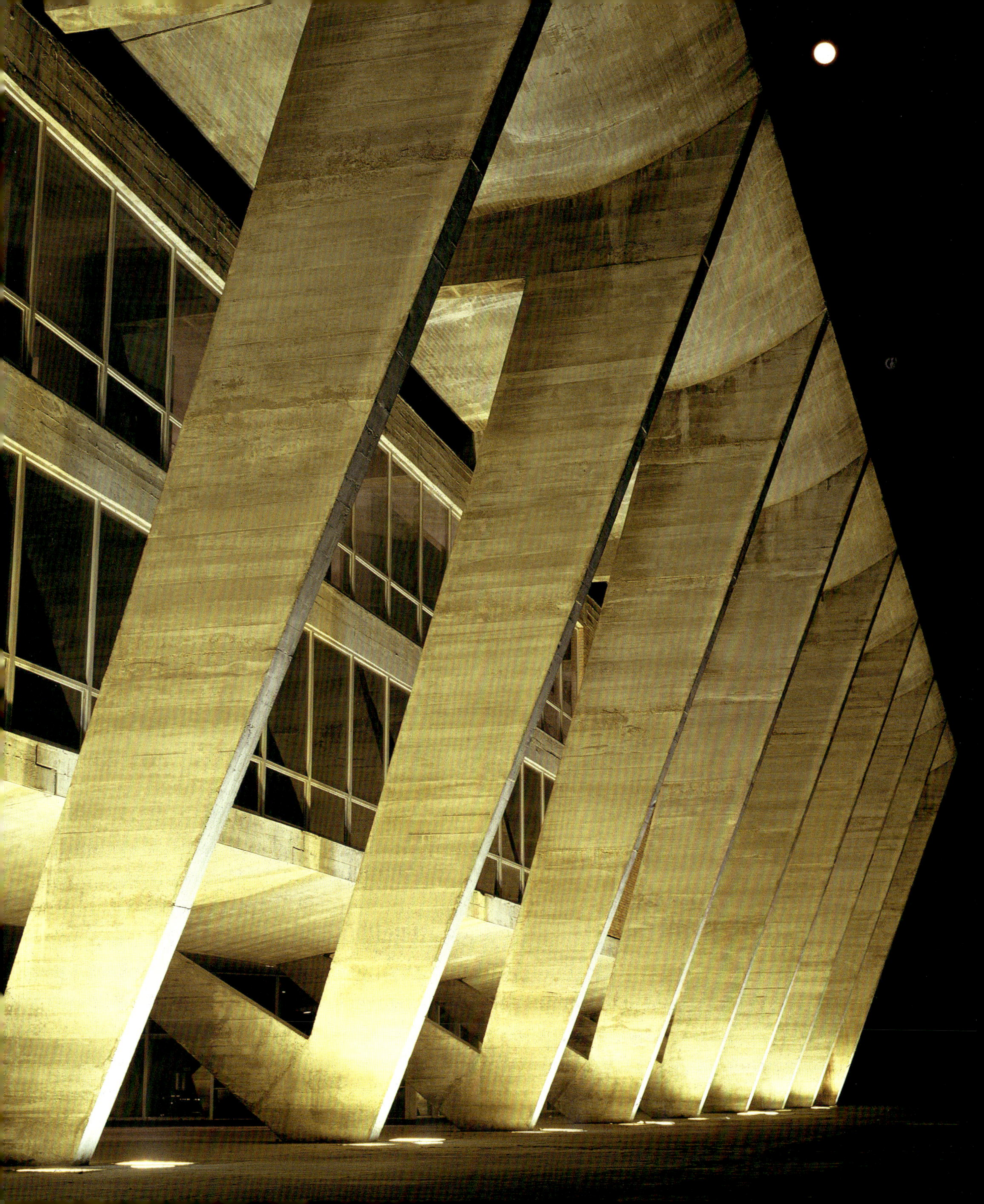

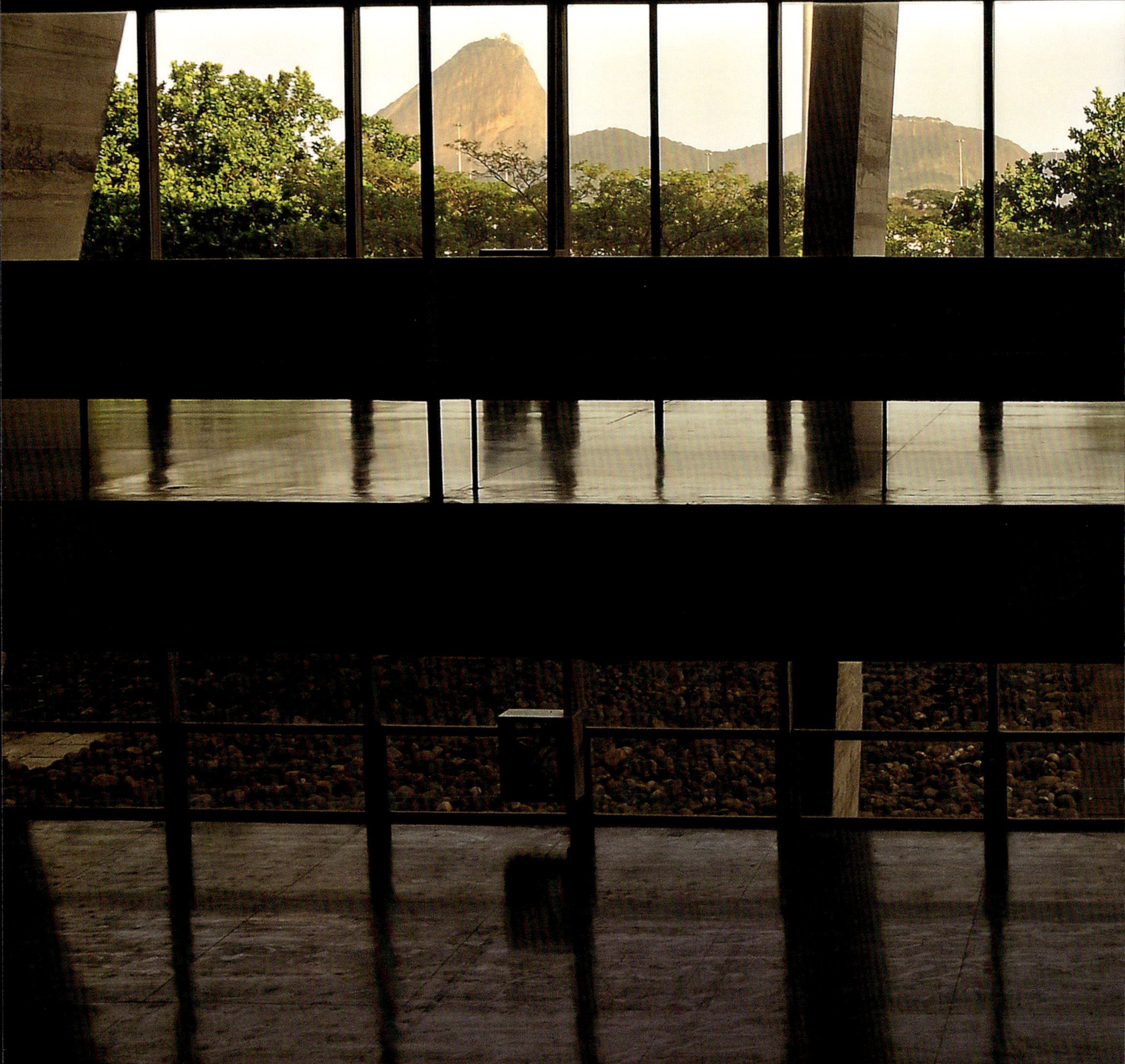

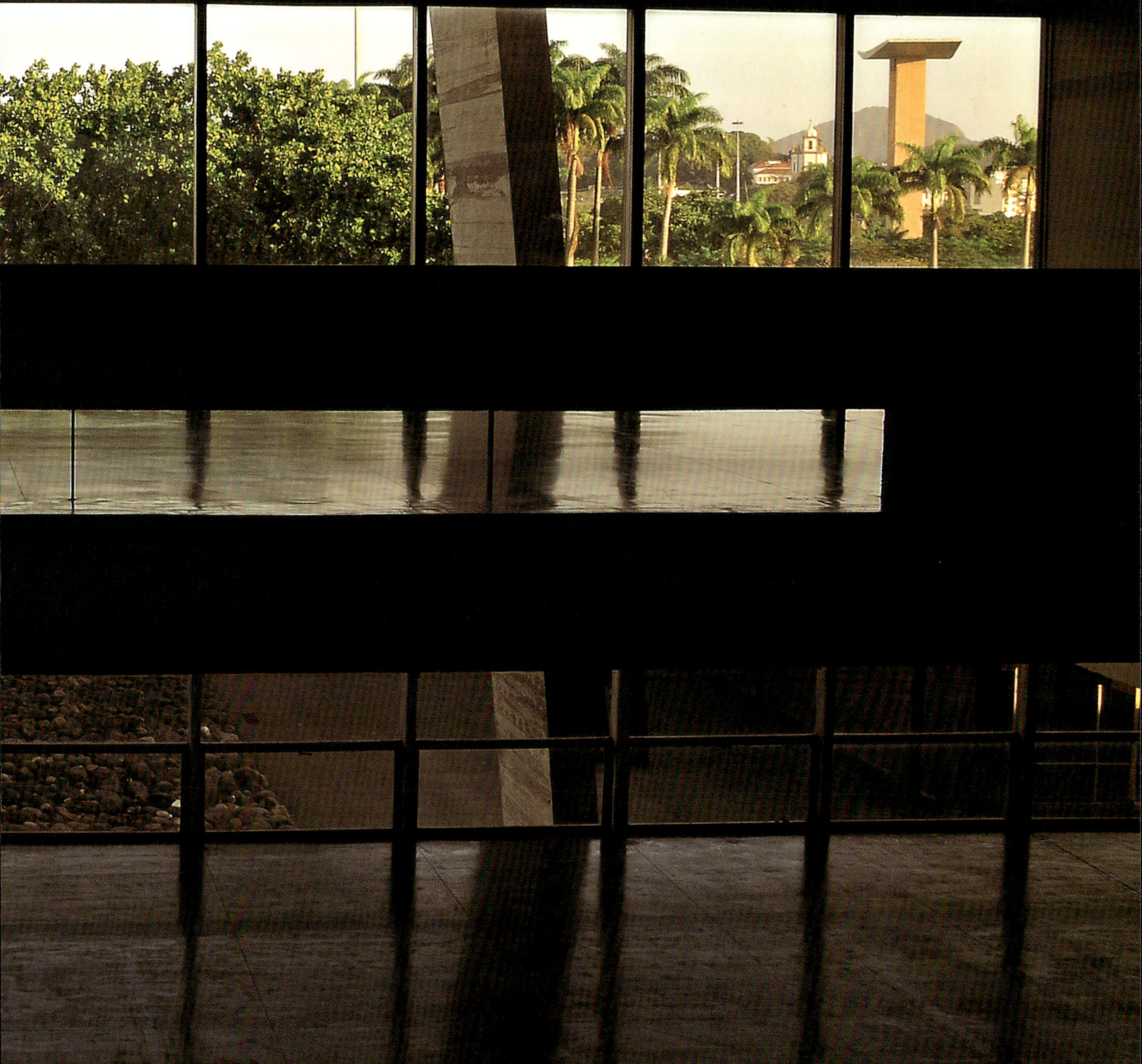

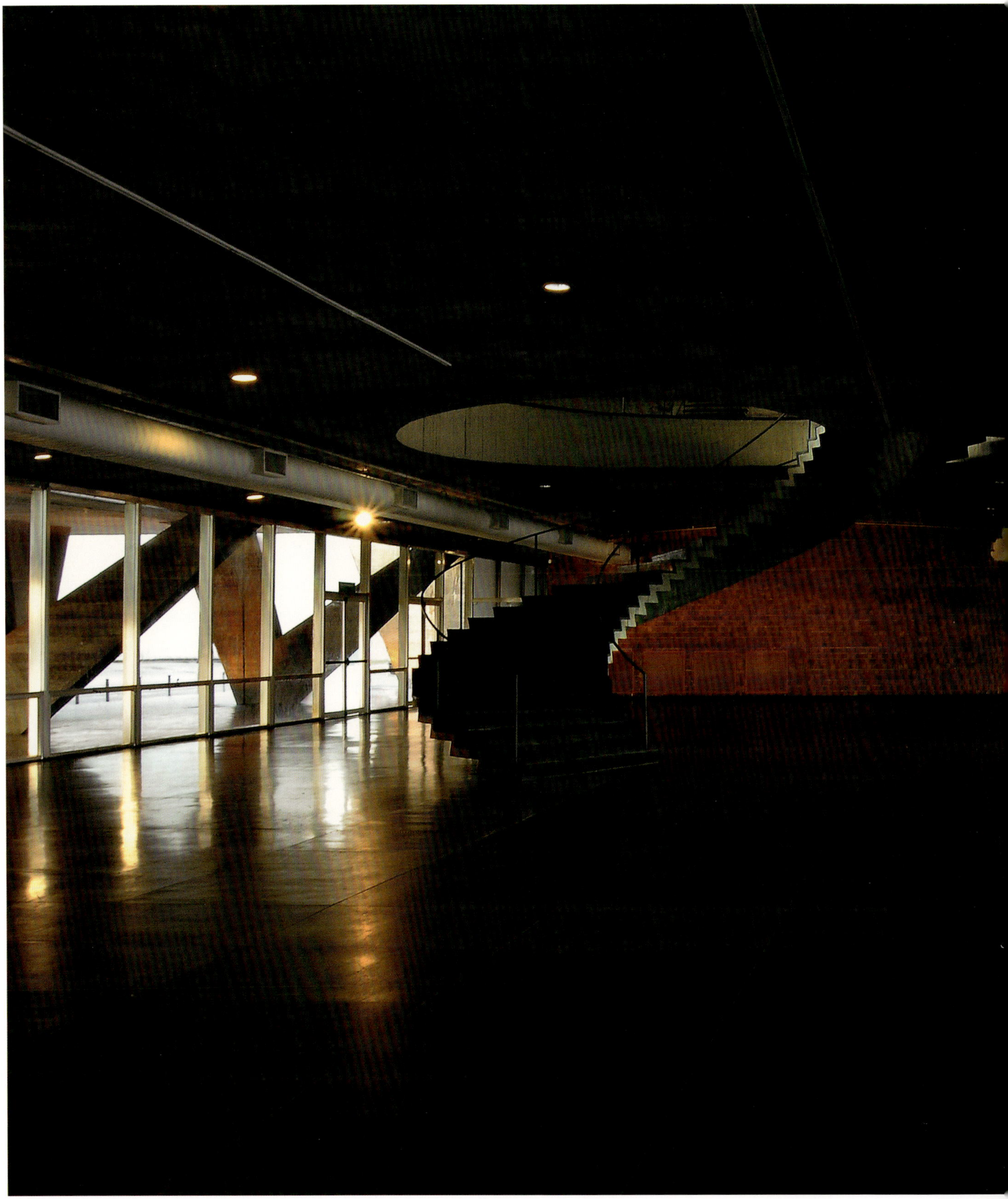

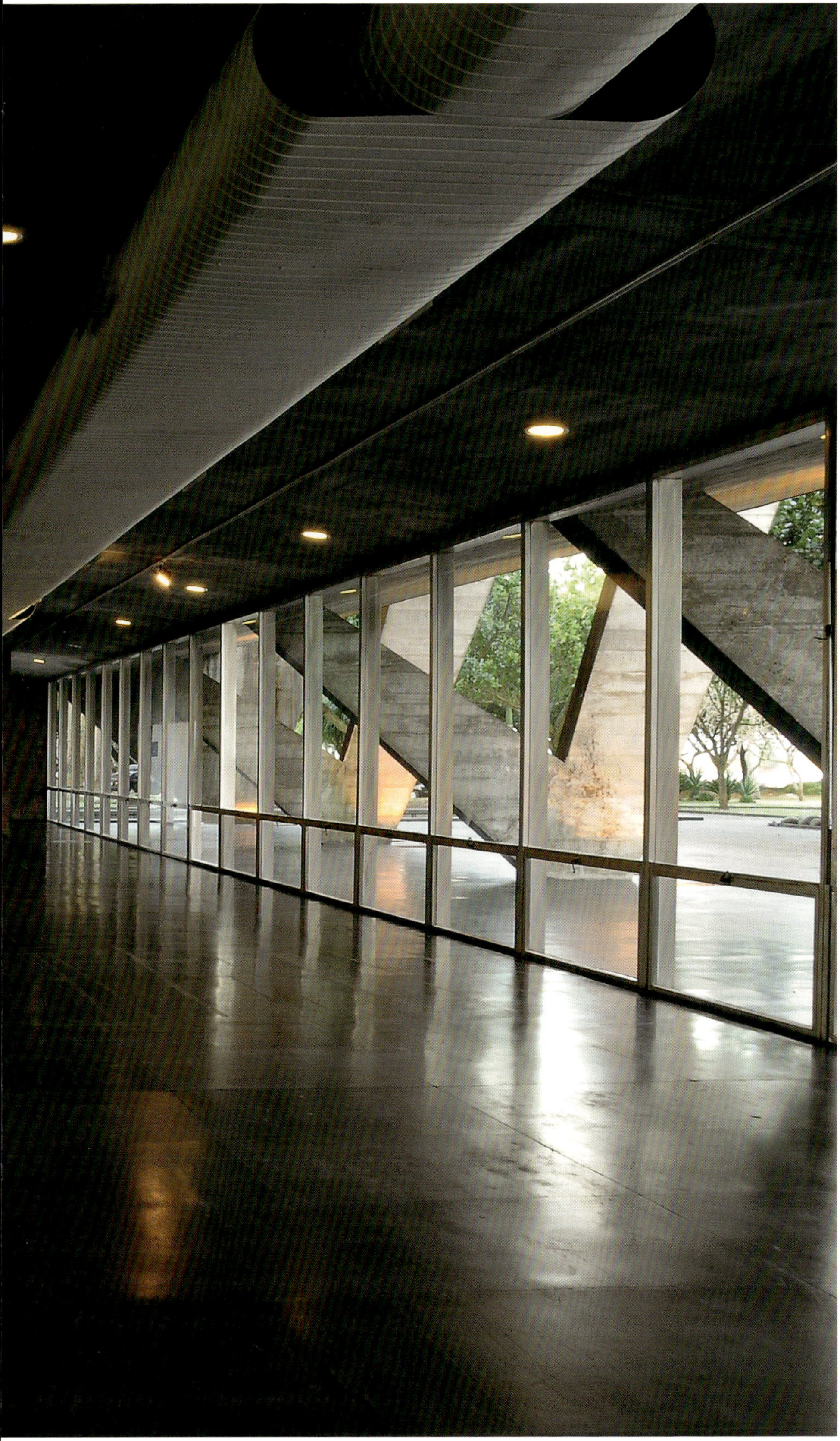

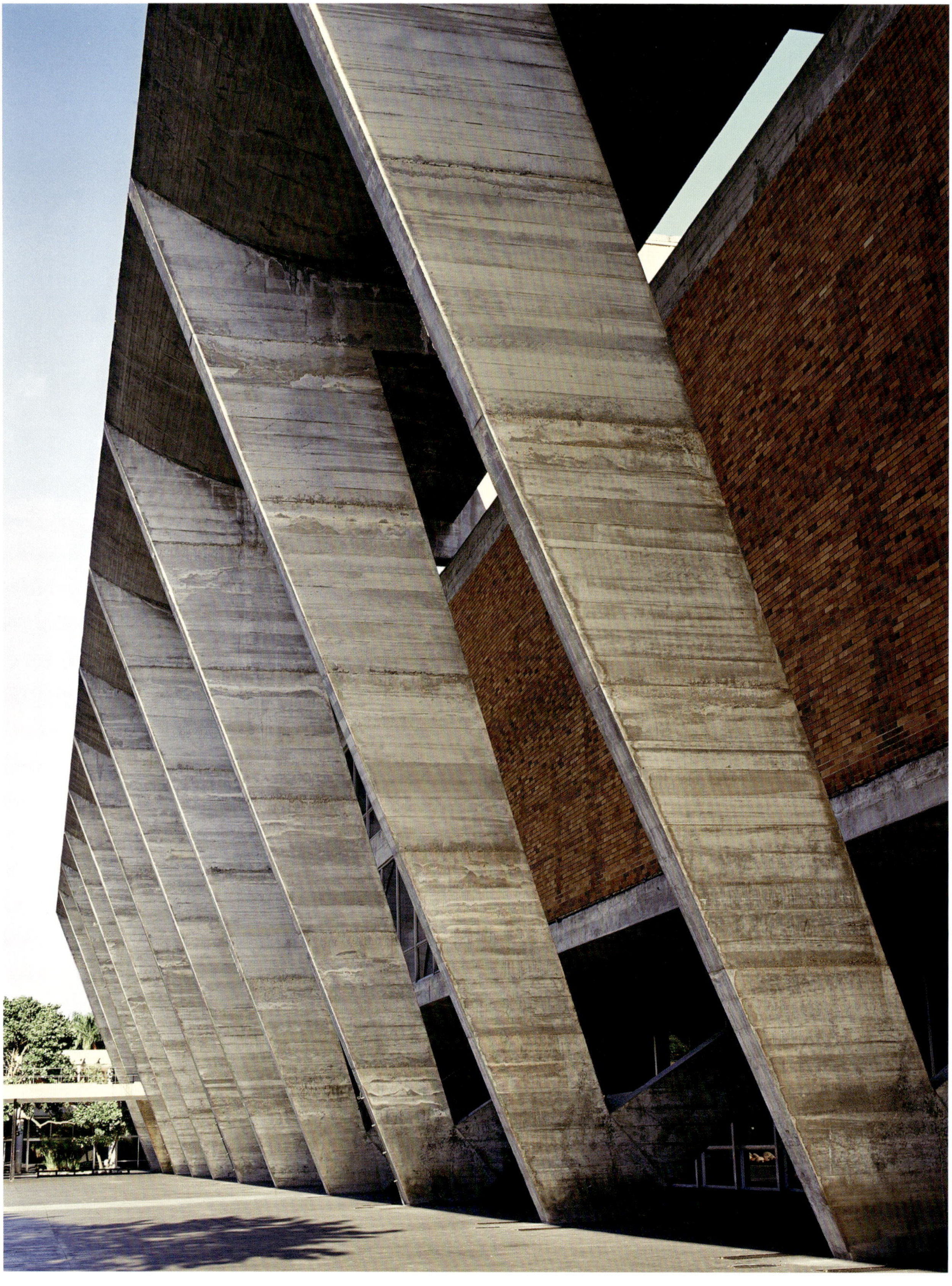

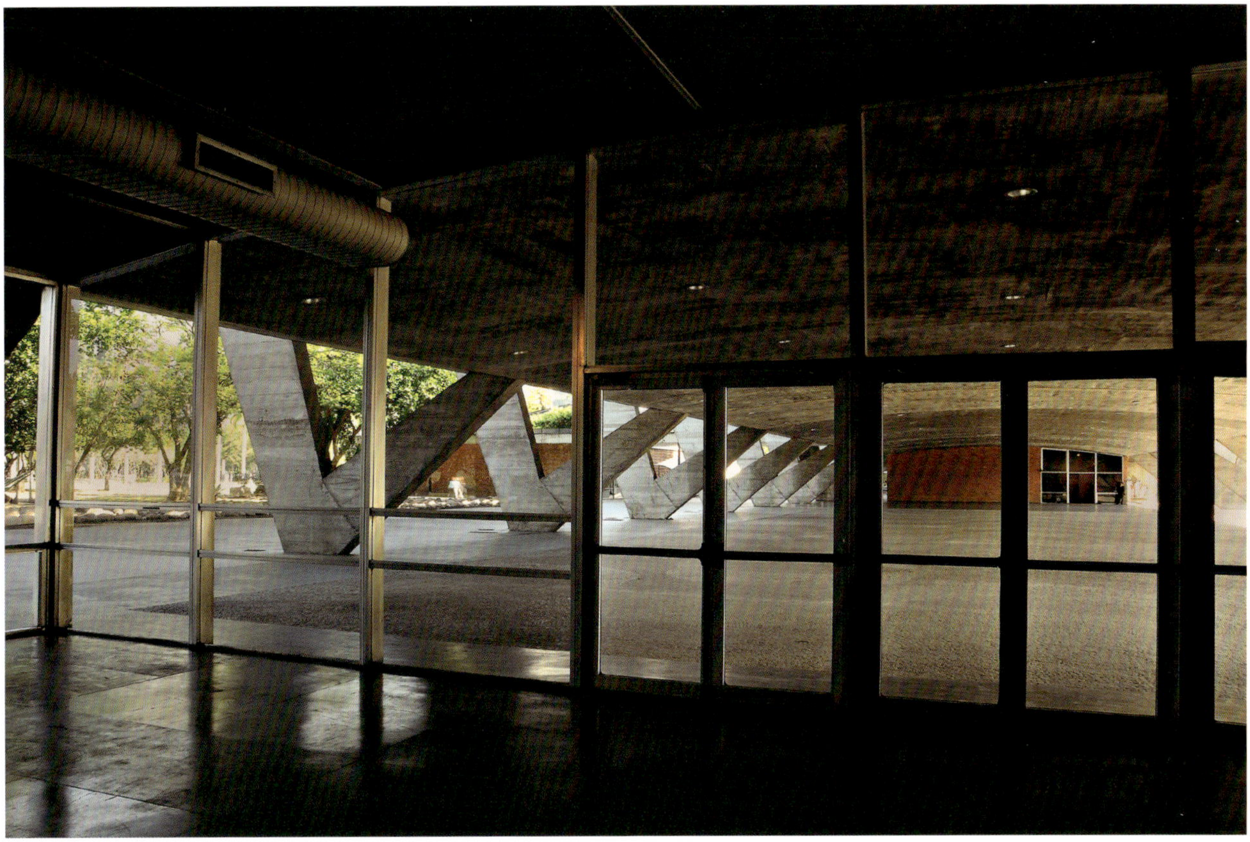

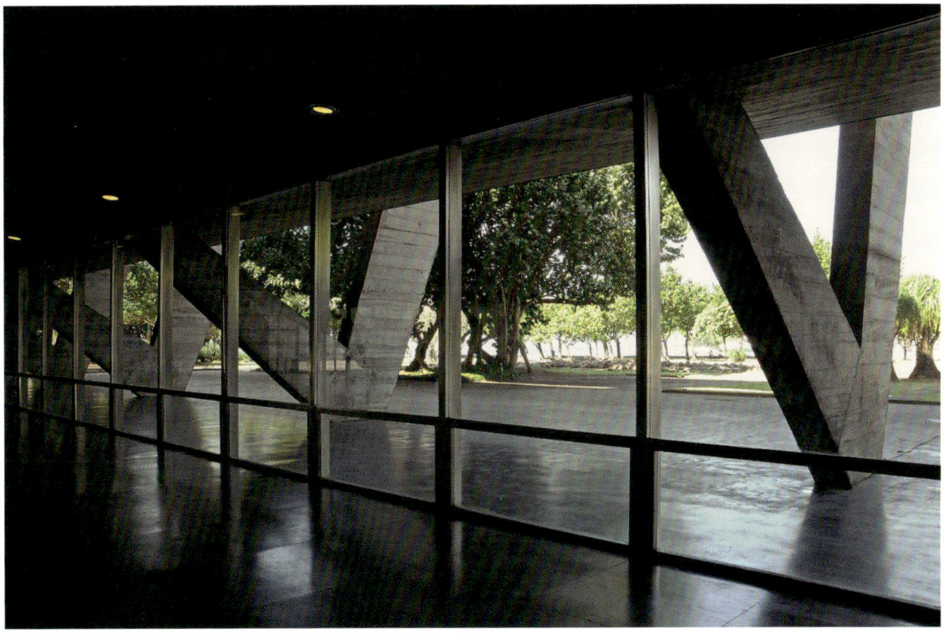

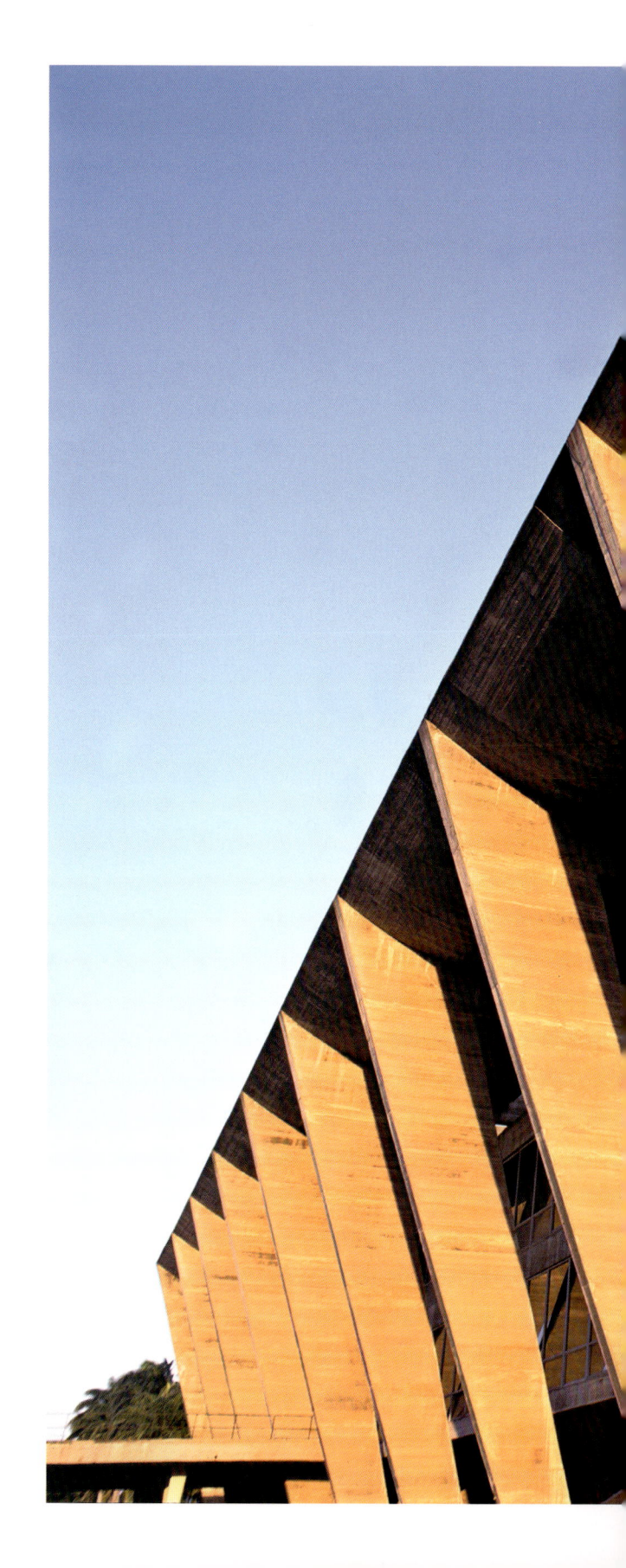

132 Museu de Arte Moderna Rio de Janeiro

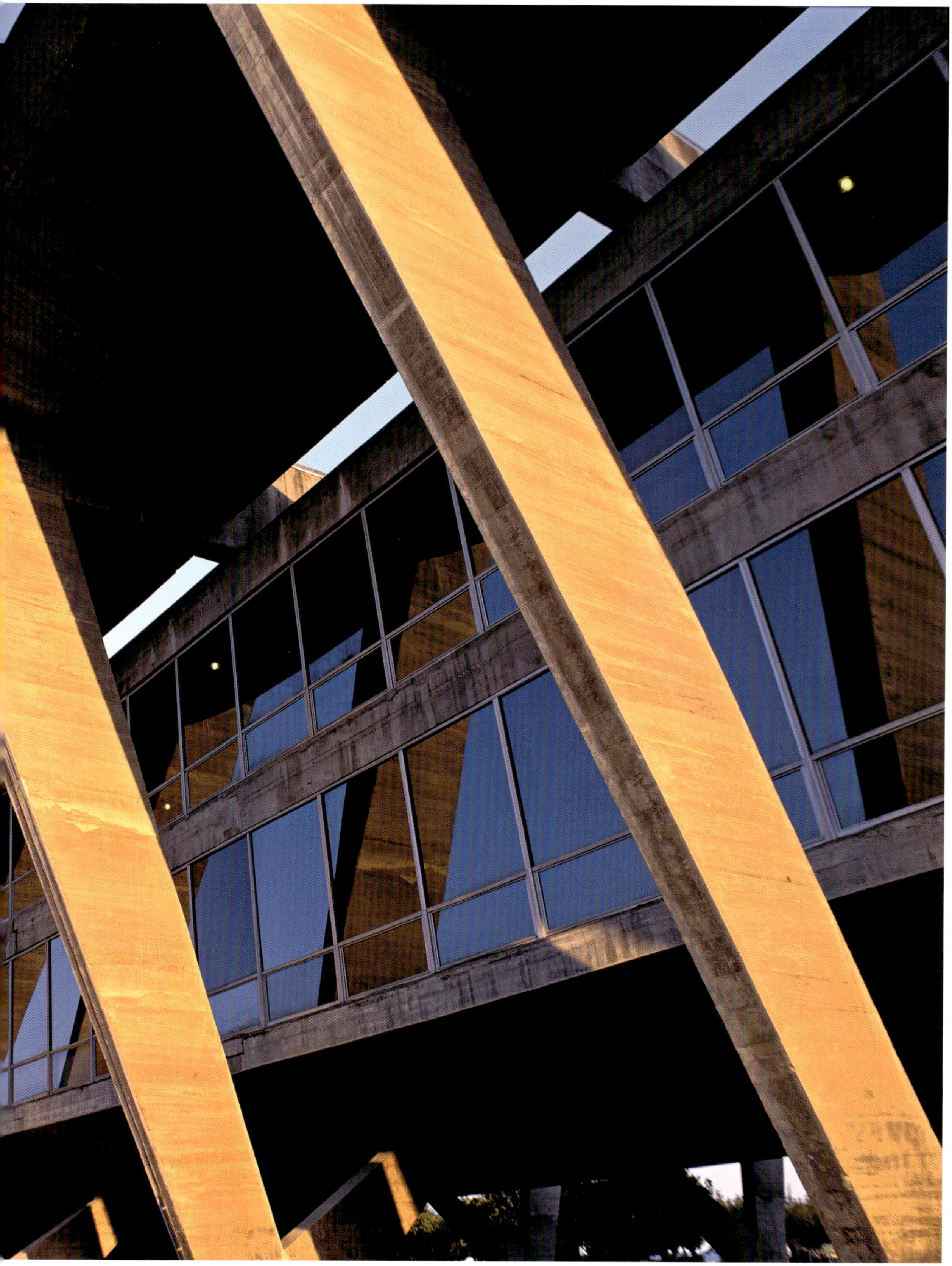

Museu de Arte Moderna Rio de Janeiro

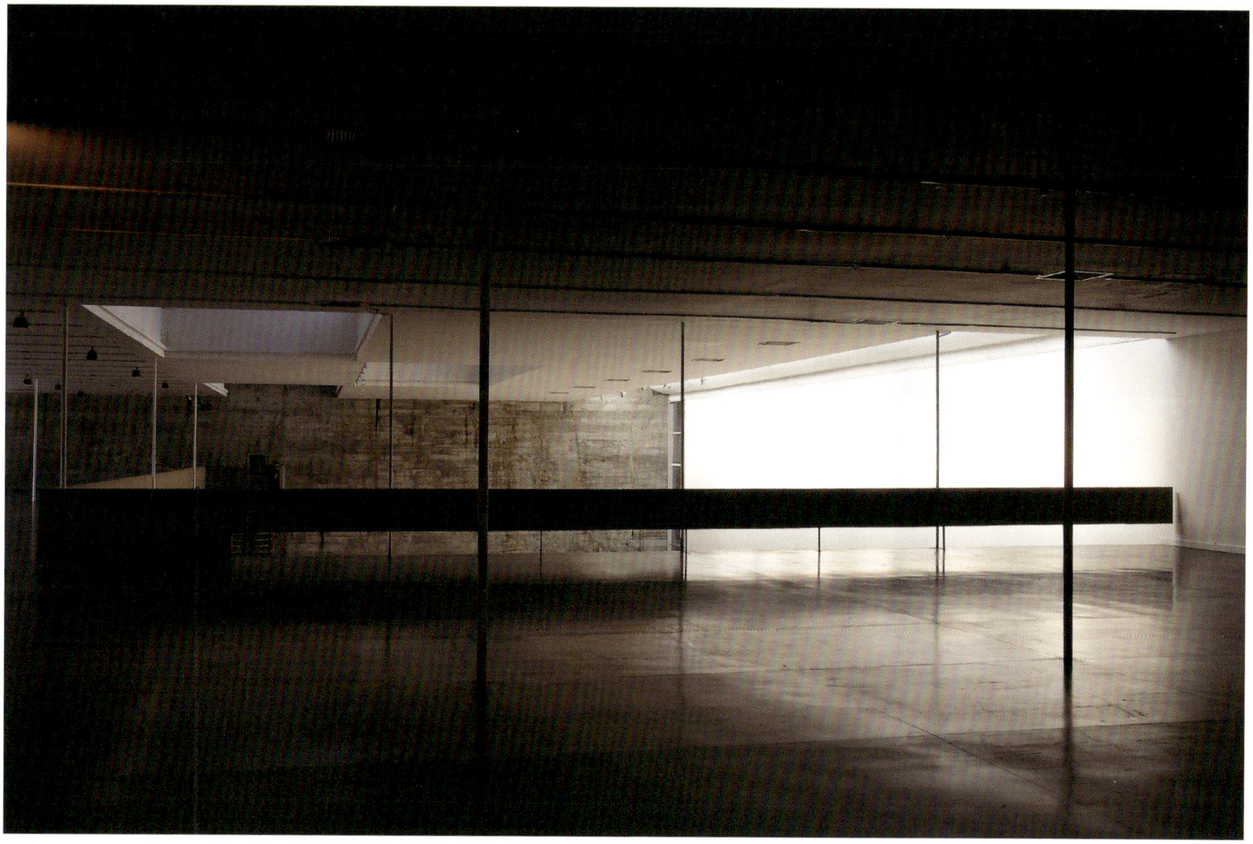

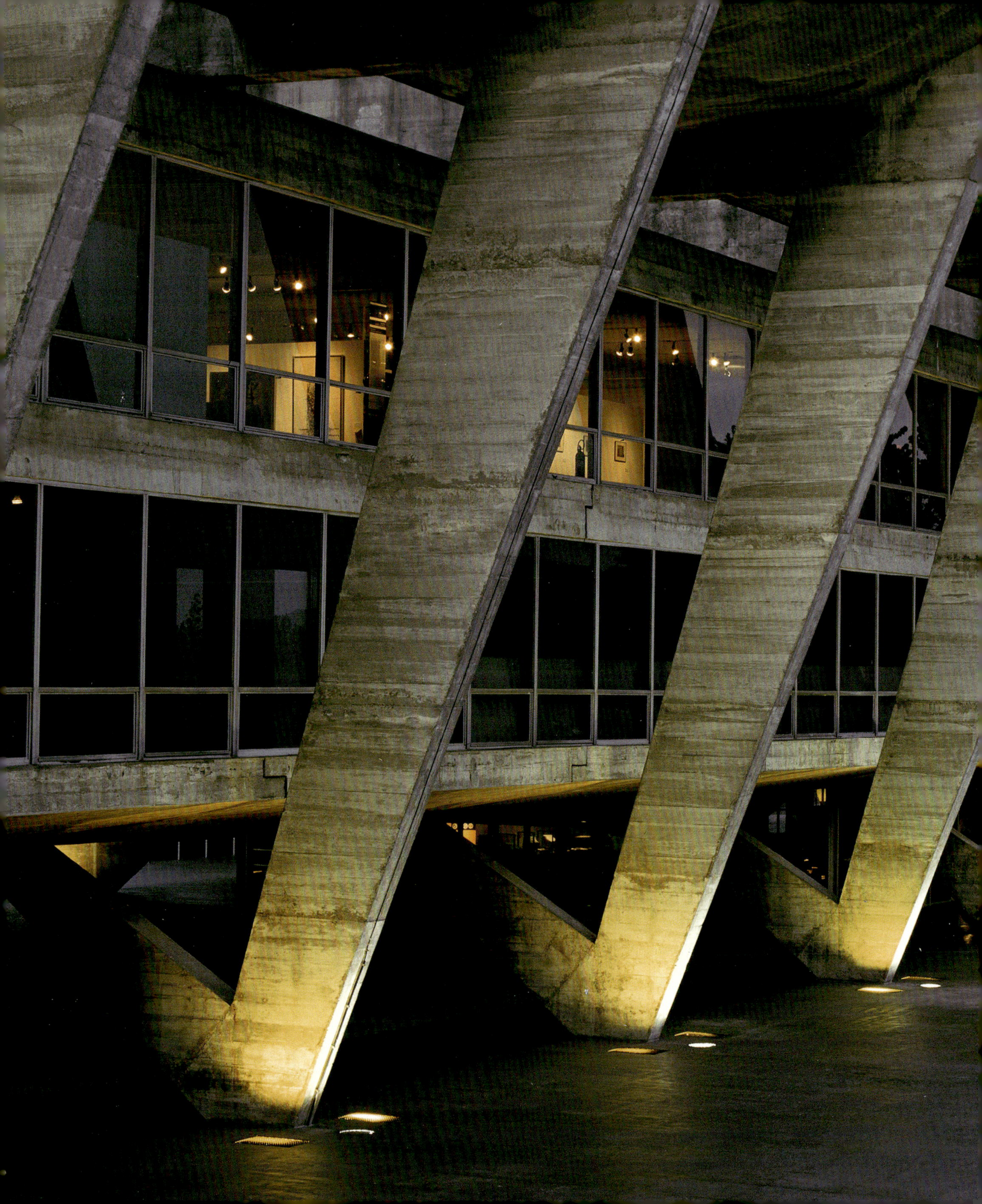

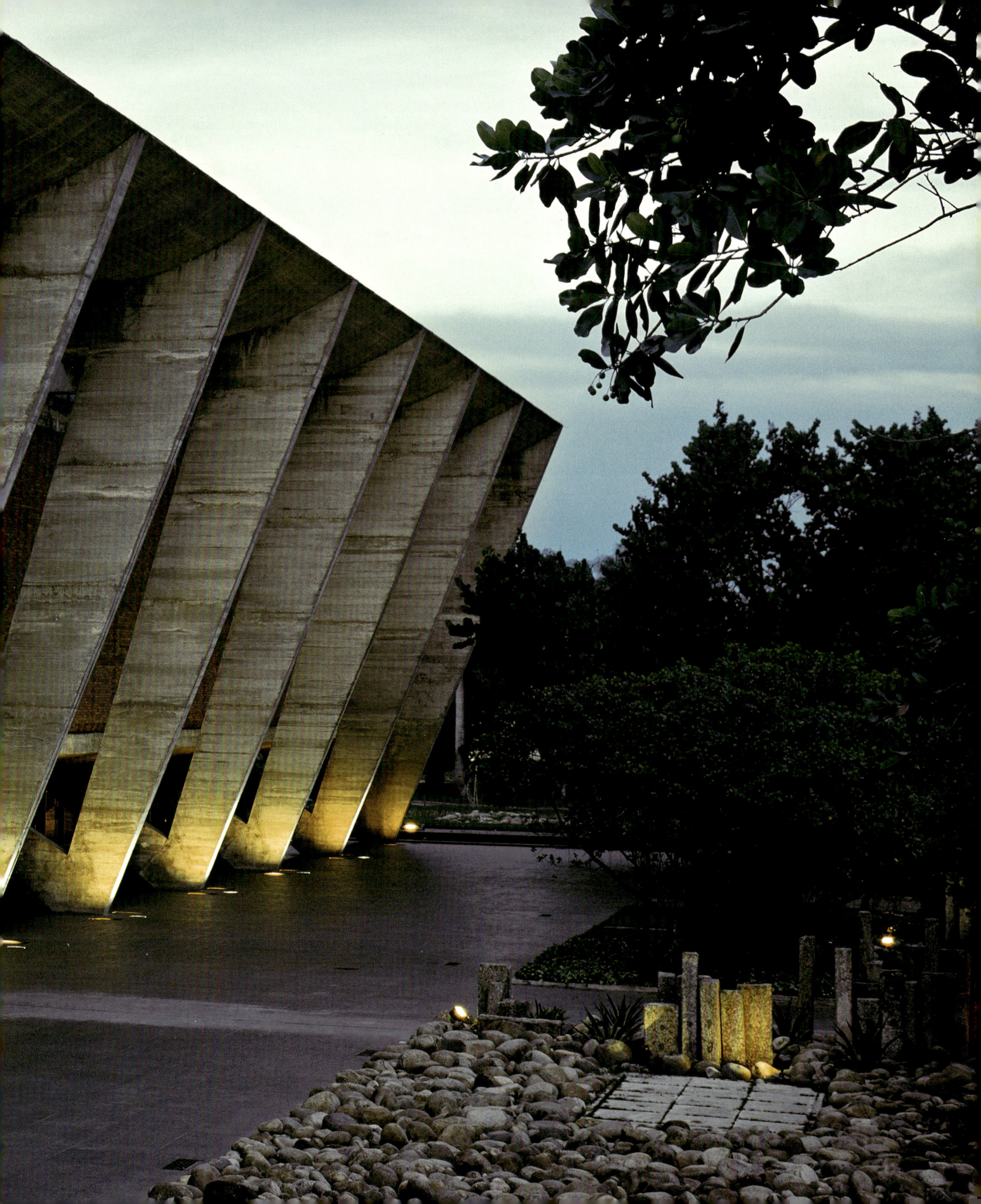

Chronology

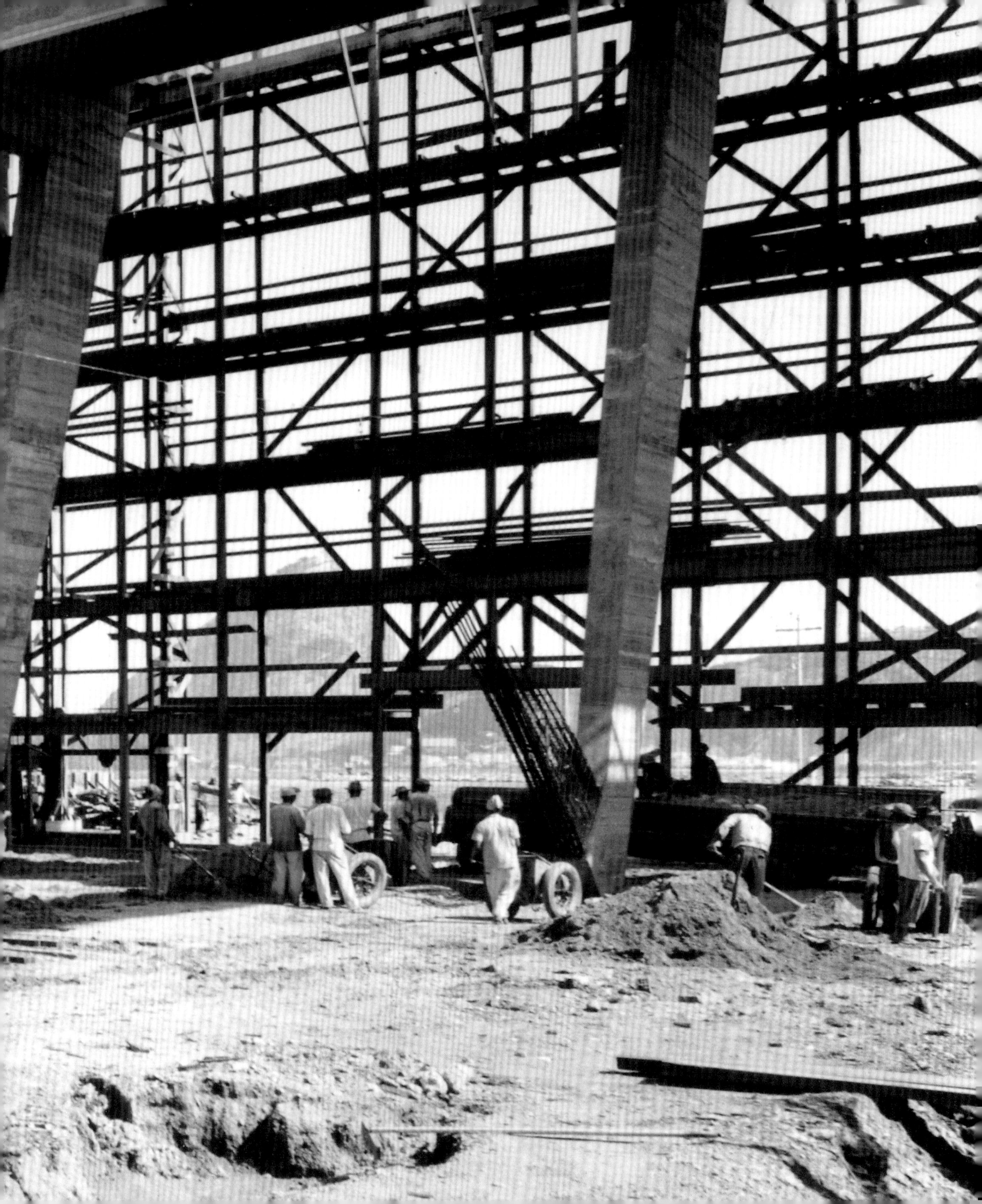

1948
The Museu de Arte Moderna do Rio de Janeiro is founded in May. Initially, it is temporarily housed in the Banco Boa Vista building located in Pio X Square, in the city Center. That same year, Affonso Eduardo Reidy, then director of the Federal District's Department of Urbanism, designs the project for the Esplanade of Santo Antônio and the Glória and Flamengo Landfill, spaces that would be occupied in six years by the MAM's permanent headquarters.

1952
The MAM is transferred to the mezzanine of the Ministry of Education and Health (currently the Gustavo Capanema Palace), where it remains until 1957. At the suggestion of the Federal District Mayor João Carlos Vital, the MAM's board of directors invites the architect Reidy to design the preliminary sketches of the Museum's permanent headquarters.

1953
A 40.000 square meter tract on the landfill Santa Luzia beach is donated by the Federal District government to the Museum. Demarcation of the tract begins for the Museum's construction. Reidy develops the architectural project and writes the Memorial in which he outlines his general concept and execution. Carmen Portinho (a member of the museum's board of directors) becomes the engineer in charge and Emilio Baumgart the mathematician. Roberto Burle Marx is invited to carry out landscaping.

1954
On September 22 the museum's board of directors and then Mayor Alim Pedro co-sign the deed that makes the donation of the tract official. On December 9, the country's then-President João Café Filho drives the foundation pile, formalizing the start of construction work. The first building to be erected is to be the School Building.

1956
Construction begins on the Exhibition Building.

1958
On January 27, the School Building is inaugurated in the presence of then Brazilian president Juscelino Kubitschek. The building becomes the Museum's headquarters, housing its administrative offices, courses and exhibitions. The first exhibition announced presents the museum's permanent collection along with the English delegation to the fourth edition of the São Paulo Biennial, including work by Ben Nicholson and British sculptors.

1962

Burle Marx and Reidy remain in the group responsible for the urbanization of the Flamengo Landfill, led by Lota Macedo Soares. Work continues on the Exhibition Building.

1964

Affonso Eduardo Reidy dies at the age of 55 without seeing his most important project concluded. His wake is held in the MAM.

1965

Brigadeiro Eduardo Gomes Park (better known as the Flamengo Landfill) is inaugurated.

1967

After 11 years, construction of the exhibition building is finally concluded. A major retrospective of work by Lasar Segall inaugurates the space.

1978

In the small hours of July 8, the exhibition building is ravaged by a fire. The museum loses part of its valuable collection and the building is damaged.

1979

The MAM is reopened to the public, with the second edition of the Salão Nacional de Artes Plásticas and embarks on a series of renovations.

1999

After a summit meeting, the MAM undergoes a series of renovations.

2005

Construction work on the Theater starts up again and is concluded in 2006 with its inauguration on November 10.

2006

With the inauguration of its Theater, the original MAM project is finally completed.

Affonso Eduardo Reidy (1909-64)

The *Carioca* Affonso Eduardo Reidy was born in Paris to a Brazilian mother and British father on October 26, 1909. His maternal grandfather was an architect and his father an engineer. As a student, he worked as intern architect and, soon afterward, as an assistant to the French urbanist Alfred Agache in elaborating the Urban Plan for the City of Rio de Janeiro. A graduate of the Escola Nacional de Belas Artes (ENBA), at a time in which urbanism was an elective and extremely under-attended course selection, he soon proved to possess a powerful urbanistic-architectural sensibility. His devotion to the profession made of him a complete architect. He experienced the heroic period of the struggle for the ENBA's modernization under the direction of Lucio Costa. Having graduated in 1930, he taught Architectural Composition (1931-33), initially as assistant to Gregori Warchavchik and, later, as Full Professor.

In 1932, as a civil servant, he was appointed chief architect of the General Office of Transportation, Labor and Construction for the Federal District. A year earlier, along with Gerson Pompeu Pinheiro, he had won the competition for the Albergue da Boa Vontade.[1] His participation in competitive examinations for public service and his work for the city – in whose employment he remained for the rest of his professional life – provided him with his most important opportunities in design and construction. In 1944 and 1945, he was vice-president of the Instituto dos Arquitetos do Brasil. From 1946 on, he was chief architect for the Department of Public Housing, created and directed by his wife, the engineer Carmen Portinho. In the years that followed, he dedicated himself to the construction of the Pedregulho Residential Complex and a series of other socially-oriented projects that earned him international recognition.

In 1948, Reidy began the re-elaboration of the Urban Plan for the City, coordinating (among other projects) the Plan for the Urbanization of the City Center, responsible for the urbanization of the esplanade that resulted from the razing of Santo Antônio Hill and the Glória and Flamengo Landfill, where the Museu de Arte Moderna do Rio de Janeiro (MAM) would eventually be built. Years later, Reidy was given the opportunity to be part of the Glória-Flamengo Landfill working group led by Lota Macedo Soares, who rendered part of his 1948 project viable. Unfortunately, Reidy died in 1964, on August 10, without seeing the completed construction.

It is no mere coincidence that the MAM, founded in 1948, before it possessed a site of its own, found shelter inside important examples of Rio de Janeiro's modern architecture: the Niemeyer-designed Banco Boa Vista was its first home, and the Ministry of Education and Health, effectively its first site, where it occupied the mezzanine from 1951 until the inauguration of the current site in 1958. Nor should it be surprising that the area donated by the city in 1954 for the museum's construction was still… sea.

Trusting that the constructed structure would act upon its users, the modern utopia, construction for the "new man" had managed to be put in practice in Brazil, and the construction of a Museum of Modern Art would be the result of such a program, as well as the search for the city's traffic and leisure solutions, materialized in Flamengo Park.

Conceived as a dialogue with the landscape – the horizontality of the composition contrasting with the outline of Rio de Janeiro's hills, the glass façades brining Burle Marx's landscaping indoors – Reidy's project is simultaneously rationalist and malleable. There is no distance between the structure and its final aspect. The free spans possess a practical purpose: the freedom of composition offered up to the exhibition space, the invitation to the garden on the ground level. From the careful use of apparent concrete to the choice of granite and Portuguese paving (of basalt and limestone), the project reaches the park.

Along with Jorge Moreira, Ernani Vasconcelos, Carlos Leão and Oscar Niemeyer, Reidy was invited by Lucio Costa to be part of the team led by Le Corbusier, which had designed and constructed the Ministry of Education and Health building in Rio de Janeiro (1937-43), a landmark of modern architecture in Brazil. At the time, Reidy became a friend and admirer of Le Corbusier and, from among the new generation of architects, he became his most faithful disciple.

Thanks to the Pedregulho's repercussion – a construction that garnered enormous national and international interest, starting with the first prize in architecture at the first edition of the São Paulo International Biennial – and to the repercussion of the Museu de Arte Moderna do Rio de Janeiro, Reidy was acclaimed as one of the most important figures in Brazilian architecture.

In the 1950s, at the invitation of the Itamaraty (the Brazilian diplomatic corps), he designed the Escola Experimental Brasil-Paraguai, built by Brazil in Asunción. In the 1960s, he took part in closed competitions for the headquarters of the World Health Organization in Geneva, and for the National Museum of Kuwait, which he won, although his project was never carried out.

His discreet presence and the fact that he had a short life – at least in comparison to his long-living peers Lucio Costa (1902-98) and Niemeyer (1907-) – may help to explain the Reidy paradox: the man responsible for our most representative public housing project and for the city's largest park is often the least-remembered of our foremost architects.

Rosana de Freitas
Curator, Center for Research and Documentation
Museu de Arte Moderna do Rio de Janeiro

1 A project of Rio de Janeiro's city hall for its department of public housing.

Image Index

p.100	Panoramic view of museum construction work integrated to Flamengo Park
p.102	Theater and northern façade of Exhibition Building, detail and theater façade
p.104	Principal façade of the theater, Exhibition Building and fountain
p.106	Gardens and southern façade of Exhibition Building with School Building in the background
p.107	Film theater auditorium
p.108	Southern façade of the Exhibition Building seen from School Building terrace, 1986
p.111	Workers preparing flagstone for School Building covering
p.117	Exhibition Building structure under construction
p.119	Pilotis and exhibition hall entrance in the background, 1986
p.123	Structure of the Exhibition Building, internal part with Guanabara Bay in the background
p.125	Façade of the Exhibition Building
p.126	View of Sugar Loaf, Glória Knoll and Monument to Brazilian Veterans from the third floor exhibition hall, 2010
p.128	View of foyer with helical stairway
p.130	Southern façade of the Exhibition Building
p.131	View of the pilotis from the foyer, administration entrance in the background and foyer view of the gardens, 2010
p.132	Façade of the Exhibition Building
p.134, 135	Exhibition hall, third floor, 2010
p.136	Southern façade of the Exhibition Building with gardens
p.139	Portico and overhang structure under construction, 1959 (detail)
p.145	School Building ramp with cobogó brickwork façade and pergola in the background

p.55	Brick and mortar placement for the School Building flagstone, 1955
p.56	Workers preparing flagstone for School Building roof
p.57	Flagstone preparation for School Building, 1956
p.58/61	View of construction, propping and concrete pouring, 1956
p.62, 63	School Building façade after concrete pouring, 1956
p.64, 65	Structure of the School Building's internal area
p.66, 67	School block flagstone waterproofing tests, 1957
p.68	Roof of the School Building with its concrete pergola, 1958
p.70	Visitors on the access ramp to the School Building terrace, internal structures and pergola, 1956
p.71	Fountain in the inner garden, 1958, and visitors standing before the School Building entrance, fountain and unfinished passageway to the Exhibition Building
p.72	View of the School Building's southern façade, 1958
p.73	Interior patio of the School Building, before placement of *cobogó* brickwork, 1958
p.74	Interior corridor and hall of the concluded School Building, 1958
p.75	Finished School Building terrace with pergola, *cobogó* brickwork on the ramp and gardens by Roberto Burle Marx
p.76	Worker standing before upper beam frame
p.77	View of construction
p.78	Frame of portico structure with School Building in the background
p.79, 80	Construction of portico structure and overhangs
p.81	Construction of portico structure and overhangs and detail of portico frames, 1958
p.82	Structuring of two interior floors of Exhibition Building
p.84	Construction of portico structure and overhangs and detail of portico frames, 1958
p.85	Construction of portico structure and overhangs, 1959
p.86	Western façade of the Exhibition Building, 1961
p.87	Detail of marquee present in one of the entrances to the Exhibition Building and partial view of the second and third floors with natural light from clerefloors
p.88	Eastern façade (with drainpipes), 1960
p.90	Partial view of second and third floors of Exhibition Building, 1960
p.91	Partial view of the monumental room, second floor, with natural lighting
p.92	Stairway that connects the second floor to the third and partial view of the second and third floors naturally lit by cleretfloors
p.93	Partial view of third floor as seen from the third with Guanabara Bay in the background
p.94	Helicoid stairway seen from the second floor and detail of structure, 1960
p.95	Helicoid stairway connecting foyer and second floor
p.96	Exhibition Building, Northern and Western façades (with drainpipes), 1961
p.98	Easter façade of the Exhibition Building and overview of the work: southern façade of the Exhibition Building with School Building in the background, 1961
p.99	Eastern façade of the Exhibition Building with marquee, 1961

p.6	Sketch of Exhibition Building structure with transversal cut
p.12	Photo of model seen from above
p.15	Photomontage with model and Guanabara Bay in background
p.18	Photomontage with model and Sugar Loaf in background
p.21	Photomontage with model and city center in background
p.23	Drawing of transversal cut of the Exhibition Building with perspective of observer
p.25	Affonso Eduardo Reidy shows model to Ludwig Grote, German delegate to the 4th edition of the São Paulo Biennial, 1957
p.27	Photo of model
p.29	Exhibition Building structure, Guanabara Bay in the background, 1958
p.30	Tractor preparing terrain for construction, 1954
p.31	Photomontage with aerial view of Guanabara Bay without the Flamengo Landfill and photomontage with aerial view of Guanabara Bay with Flamengo Landfill, 1954
p.32	Razing of Santo Antônio Hill, 1954
p.33	Trucks transporting earth from Santo Antônio Hill to the construction lot and razing of Santo Antônio Hill, 1954
p.34	View of terrain demarcated for construction and unloading earth, 1955
p.35	Worker on tractor preparing terrain for construction, 1955
p.36	Back of construction office with city center in the background, 1955
p.37	Views of terrain for construction with Guanabara Bay in the background, 1954, and Affonso Eduardo Reidy and Carmen Portinho with group on the day the last construction pile was driven, 1955
p.38	Franki piles barracks, 1954, and construction workers, 1955
p.39	Construction of barracks, 1957
p.40	View of steam-driven pile drivers with city center in the background, 1955
p.41	View of steam-driven pile drivers with Guanabara Bay in the background, 1955
p.42, 43	Workers preparing concrete foundations, 1955
p.44	Transporting beams for pile weight test, 1955
p.45	Museum sign with pile driver in the background and construction workers pouring concrete, 1955
p.46	Workers mixing concrete, 1955
p.47	Workers pouring concrete and operating mixer, 1955
p.48	Workers carrying frames, 1955
p.49	Frames for school building columns, 1955
p.50	Workers preparing construction foundations, 1955
p.51	Affonso Eduardo Reidy participates in the concrete pouring process for the exhibition building alongside workers and worker with frames, 1955
p.52, 53	Views of construction work with Guanabara Bay in the background, 1955
p.54	Preparing basement frames for concrete pouring, 1955

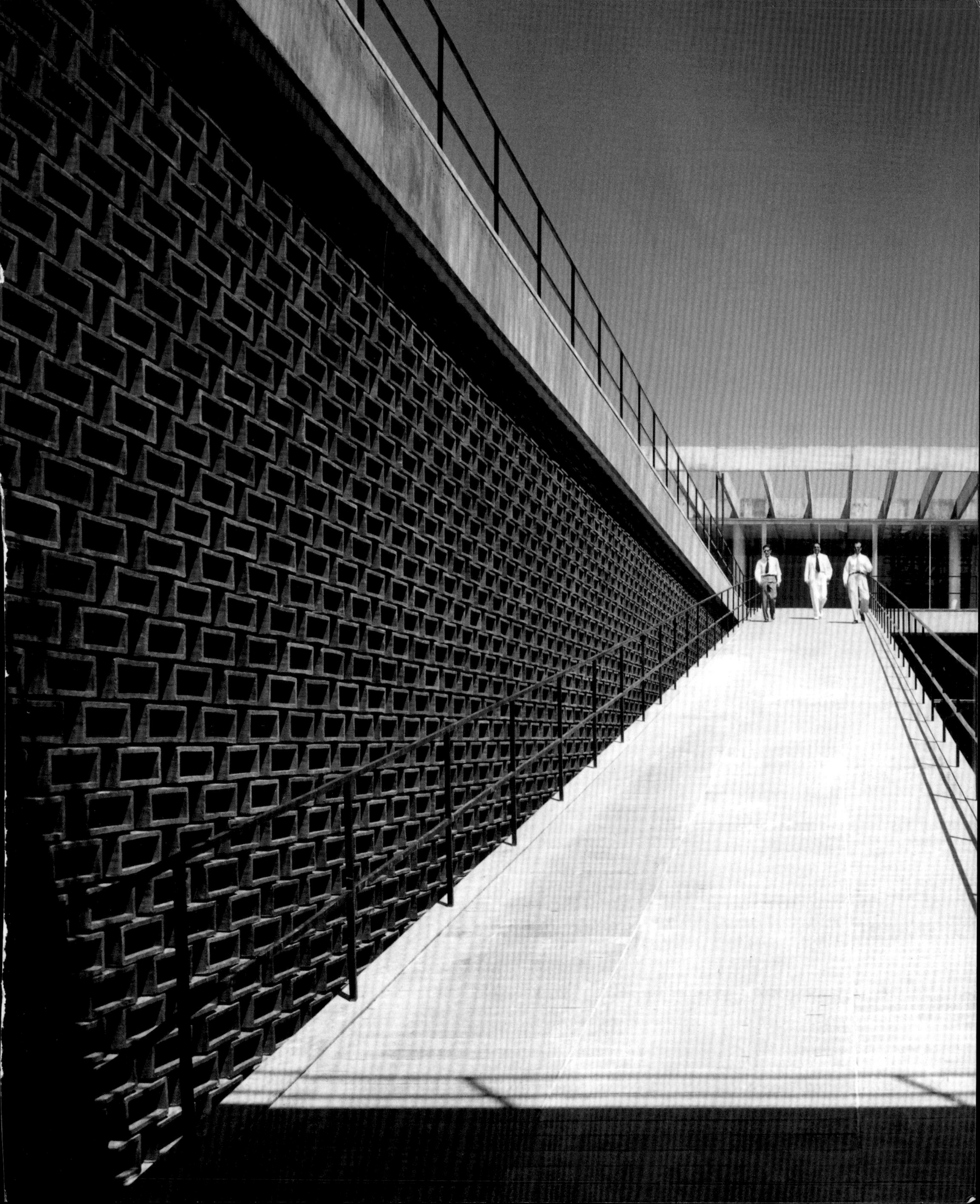

Publishers
Isabel Diegues
Ricardo Sardenberg

Editor
Frederico Coelho

Editorial Assistant
Vanessa Gouveia

Graphic Design and Layout
Carla Marins
Mariana Mansur
Mariana Boghossian

Translation
Stephen Berg

Proofreading
Renato Rezende

Final Proofreading
Eduardo Carneiro

Cobogó Team
Melina Bial
Ronaldo Pinheiro
Lívia Lima

Image Treatment
Trio Studio

Printing
Gráfica Santa Marta

Cover photograph
Aertsens Michel (detail) MAM collection

Photographs
Page 31 Carlos Botelho (top) and Jerry (bottom)
Pages 68, 72, 73, 80, 82, 85/88, 90, 94/96, 98 Aertsens Michel
Page 75 Marcel Gautherot
Page 76 Agência Fotográfica Vasclo
Pages 108, 119 Geraldo Viola
Pages 100/106 César Barreto
Pages 107, 125/137 Vicente de Mello

These and all other images in this book are part of the
MAM Center for Documentation and Research Collection.

Every possible effort has been made to identify authorship of the images in this book.
In spite of this, some photographers were not located, as was the case with some
of the individuals in the photographs. We are prepared to give credit to all who claim it.

All rights reserved Editora de Livros Cobogó Ltda.
Rua Jardim Botânico, 635/406
Rio de Janeiro – RJ – 22470-050
www.cobogo.com.br

2011 © Copyright the authors
2011 © Copyright Editora de Livros Cobogó

CIP-BRASIL. CATALOGAÇÃO-NA-FONTE
SINDICATO NACIONAL DOS EDITORES
DE LIVROS, RJ

M974
Museu de Arte Moderna Rio de Janeiro : architecture and construction / [edited by Frederico Coelho] ; [translated by Stephen Berg]. - Rio de Janeiro : Cobogó, 2011.
il.

Texts in English
Includes bibliography
ISBN 978-85-60965-16-8

1. Reidy, Affonso Eduardo, 1909-1964.
2. Museu de Arte Moderna do Rio de Janeiro.
3. Art museum architecture - Rio de Janeiro (RJ).
4. Art museums - Projects and construction.
5. Modern architecture - 20th century - Brazil.
6. Architecture - Rio de Janeiro (RJ) - History - 19th century. I. Coelho, Frederico.

11-1634.   CDD: 727.7098153
           CDU: 727:069(815.3)

Museu de Arte Moderna
Rio de Janeiro

Av. Infante Dom Henrique 85
Parque do Flamengo
20021-140 Rio de Janeiro RJ Brasil
www.mamrio.org.br

Sponsors
Petrobras
Light

Partners
Bolsa de Arte do Rio de Janeiro
Credit Suisse Hedging-Griffo
Gávea Investimentos
Investidor Profissional
Mica Mídia Cards
Outback Steakhouse
Revista Piauí
Salta Elevadores

Lei de Incentivo à Cultura | Ministério da Cultura

Special Projects
Biblioteca Aquisição de Mobiliário e Equipamentos, Secretaria de Estado de Cultura
Cinemateca Aquisição de Acervo e Digitalização de Acervo Documental, ONS Operador Nacional do Sistema Elétrico
Núcleo Experimental de Educação e Arte, Unimed e Petrobras
TAM, Transportadora oficial do MAM

President
Carlos Alberto Gouvêa Chateaubriand

Vice-President
João Maurício de Araujo Pinho Filho

Director
Luiz Schymura

Counselors
Armando Strozenberg
Carlos Alberto Gouvêa Chateaubriand
Demósthenes M. de Pinho Filho
Eduardo Vianna
Elisabete Carneiro Floris
Gilberto Chateaubriand President
Heitor Reis
Helio Portocarrero
Henrique Luz
Irapoan Cavalcanti de Lyra
João Maurício de Araujo Pinho Vice-president
João Maurício de Araujo Pinho Filho
Joaquim Paiva
José Luiz Alquéres
Kátia Mindlin Leite Barbosa
Luis Antonio de Almeida Braga
Luiz Carlos Barreto
Luiz Schymura
Nelson Eizirik
Paulo Albert Weyland Vieira

Visual Arts
Luiz Camillo Osório Curator
Frederico Coelho Assistant

Museology
Cláudia Calaça Coordinator
Veronica Cavalcante
Cátia Louredo
Fátima Noronha

Production
Hugo Bianco
Renata Contins

Press Liaison
CW&A Comunicação

Design
Carla Marins Coordinator
Mariana Boghossian Trainee

Setting Up
Cosme de Souza
José Marcelo Peçanha
Rafael dos Santos Campos

Exhibition Hall
Alessandro Hage
Marcio Andre Oliveira
Evelin Cristina Damascena Lima
Rodrigo de Lima Rosa
Terezinha Silva de Oliveira
José Luiz Nery Filho

Research and Documentation
Rosana de Freitas Curator
Adriano Braz
Claudio Barbosa
Mauricio Sales de Brito
Elizabeth Varela
Verônica Sá Ferreira

Film Archive
Gilberto Santeiro Curator
Hernani Heffner Assistant
Carlos Eduardo Pereira
João Roberto Costa
José Quental
Sidney de Mattos

Operations and Events
Cláudio Roberto

Maintenance
Behar Engenharia

Management and Finances
Henrique Andrade Oliveira Coordinator
Cláudio Pereira
Eduardo Gomes Chaves
Sandra Borges dos Santos
Leandro Oliveira de Souza
Edson Gomes dos Santos Jr.

Reception
Tânia Nascimento
Fabiana Lima
Janaina Amorim dos Santos

Cleaness
Adriana da Silva Pereira
José Geraldo Avelino
Juarez Lacerda Leal
Luiz Carlos dos Santos
Neuza Costa Pinheiro
Tereza Cristina Vasconcelos
Glayton Amaral Lisboa
Carlos Magno Silva Leocádio

Security
Transegur Vigilância e Segurança

This book was set in Avenir and Minion.
Printed by Gráfica Santa Marta
on 150 g/m² matte couche paper
for Editora Cobogó.